The ADD Hyperactivity Workbook for Parents, Teachers, and Kids

Harvey C. Parker, Ph.D.

Specialty Press, Inc.

Parker, Harvey C.
    The ADD Hyperactivity Workbook
    for Parents, Teachers, and Kids
    p. 142

    Summary: Effective strategies for identifying and
managing children with attention deficit disorders at home
and in schools.

ISBN 0-9621629-6-5

  1. Attention deficit disorder-Treatment
2. Hyperactivity-Treatment

Published by Specialty Press, Inc.
(formerly Impact Publications, Inc.)
Suite 102
300 Northwest 70th Avenue
Plantation, Florida 33317
(305) 792-8944

Manufactured in the United States of America

To Roberta, Michelle, and Julie.
Thank you for your love, patience
and support.

Table of Contents

GOAL CARD PROGRAM (I)ntermediate
Grades One - Eight

Child's Name_____ Teacher _____

Grade_____ School _____ Home Room _____

Week of _____

Goal Card

	MON	TUE	WED	THU	FRI
1. Paid attention in class					
2. Completed work in class					
3. Completed homework					
4. Was well behaved					
5. Desk & notebook neat					
Totals					
Teacher's Initials					

Rating Scales

N/A = Not Applicable
0 = Losing, Forgetting or
   Destroying Card
CHECK SCALE TO BE USED

____   ____

1 = Terrible   1 = Poor
2 = Poor   2 = Better
3 = Fair   3 = Good
4 = Good
5 = Excellent

Try For _____ Points

- -

Child's Name_____ Teacher _____

Grade_____ School _____ Home Room _____

Week of _____

Goal Card

	MON	TUE	WED	THU	FRI
1. Paid attention in class					
2. Completed work in class					
3. Completed homework					
4. Was well behaved					
5. Desk & notebook neat					
Totals					
Teacher's Initials					

Rating Scales

N/A = Not Applicable
0 = Losing, Forgetting or
   Destroying Card
CHECK SCALE TO BE USED

____   ____

1 = Terrible   1 = Poor
2 = Poor   2 = Better
3 = Fair   3 = Good
4 = Good
5 = Excellent

Try For _____ Points

GOAL CARD PROGRAM (I)ntermediate
Grades One - Eight

Child's Name_____ Teacher _____

Grade_____ School _____ Home Room _____

Week of _____

Goal Card

	MON	TUE	WED	THU	FRI
1. Paid attention in class					
2. Completed work in class					
3. Completed homework					
4. Was well behaved					
5. Desk & notebook neat					
Totals					
Teacher's Initials					

Rating Scales

N/A = Not Applicable
0 = Losing, Forgetting or Destroying Card
CHECK SCALE TO BE USED

____	____
1 = Terrible	1 = Poor
2 = Poor	2 = Better
3 = Fair	3 = Good
4 = Good	
5 = Excellent	

Try For _____ Points

- -

Child's Name_____ Teacher _____

Grade_____ School _____ Home Room _____

Week of _____

Goal Card

	MON	TUE	WED	THU	FRI
1. Paid attention in class					
2. Completed work in class					
3. Completed homework					
4. Was well behaved					
5. Desk & notebook neat					
Totals					
Teacher's Initials					

Rating Scales

N/A = Not Applicable
0 = Losing, Forgetting or Destroying Card
CHECK SCALE TO BE USED

____	____
1 = Terrible	1 = Poor
2 = Poor	2 = Better
3 = Fair	3 = Good
4 = Good	
5 = Excellent	

Try For _____ Points

Chapter One
Characteristics of Children with Attention Deficit Disorder

Introduction

Hardly a week goes by that there isn't one article or another published in a local newspaper or national magazine on the topic of attention deficit disorder (ADD). Television talk show hosts have addressed the topic and professional journals and texts in psychology and medicine contain numerous research papers on the disorder. Parent support groups have been formed throughout the United States, Canada, and other countries to assist families by providing a forum by which parents can exchange information and experiences about raising a hyperactive, inattentive child.

Perhaps some of the fervor about ADD has to do with the medication controversy that had surrounded the treatment of these children. Perhaps interest in the disorder was generated by parents who are standing up on behalf of their children to see to it that their rights to a quality education are ensured. Perhaps more attention is being paid to ADD because we've come to realize that it has very important long range consequences as we now know that a substantial number of children with ADD will grow up to be adults with ADD. Whatever the reason is for all this interest, it can only do some good. It's hard enough to raise a child or teenager these days. It's very hard to raise one who has an attention deficit disorder. Both the parents of children with ADD, and the children themselves, can use some help.

This workbook was designed to give practical information to parents and teachers about ADD and related problems. This chapter and the following two chapters provide an overview of these disorders describing the characteristics of children with ADD as well as an explanation of possible causes and a description of established treatments. The remaining chapters provide hands-on training to assist parents and teachers in managing aspects of the disorder at home and in school. Worksheets are included to refine the reader's skill in applying behavioral strategies to child management. Suggestions are offered to help teachers make classroom accommodations which could help students with ADD perform better in school. There's also a story to read with the child who has ADD to encourage a positive sense of self-esteem and a better understanding of the disorder.

Most parents of children with ADD feel quite alone. They often think that the problems they and their child experience are unique to them. Mothers, in particular, and especially mothers of young children with ADD, feel estranged from other parents. It is not uncommon for them to report feeling sadness, isolation, and self-doubt about their ability to raise their child. Interestingly, when they meet other parents of children with ADD an immediate bond is formed and they get comfort in knowing they are not alone.

Parents of children with ADD describe very similar experiences.

"Whenever we go out to a restaurant my husband and I spend most of our time reminding Jessica to sit still. She's just impossible to take anywhere. She's always going ninety miles an hour."

"Robert just got his drivers' license eight months ago and already he's gotten two tickets and was involved in one accident. He's always in a rush and doesn't seem to think things out before acting."

"I never know what to expect when I pick Steven up at school. I can't believe he's only four and already, everyday he gets a bad report from the teacher. I feel like it's my fault. Just once I'd like to pick him up and see his teacher smiling at me."

"My husband and I can't understand it. We fought with Allison all last night to do her homework. First she didn't remember what to do for homework. Then, when we figured out what the assignment was, she didn't know how to do it. After a two hour struggle we finally got it finished. To top it off, this afternoon we got a call from her teacher who told us that she didn't hand it in."

Most parents take their children's behavior for granted. For example, when they go to a movie, they generally anticipate their children will become absorbed in the movie and watch quietly, perhaps asking once in a while for a refreshment. On shopping trips most children tag along with their parents, occasionally getting impatient and out of hand. When most parents go to open school night they generally look forward to seeing their child's classroom and are optimistic that they'll be greeted warmly with a good report from their youngster's teacher. While such positive experiences are commonplace for most parents, they are often quite uncommon for parents of children with ADD.

There have been thousands of scientific articles about hyperactivity and attention deficits in children published in professional journals. However, up until the past few years parents did not have many resources available to them for accurate information. Health-care professionals were often unaware of the scientific literature on the topic and children with ADD were often undiagnosed or misdiagnosed by physicians and mental health professionals. Some regarded them as learning disabled, emotionally disturbed, or the product of an unhealthy diet or poor parenting. Errors in diagnosis led to mistakes in treatment and many parents of children with ADD wasted time and money on unsuccessful therapies, often ending up no better after lengthy treatment than when they first started. We have become much better educated about ADD in the last few years and myths and misconceptions about this condition are being shattered. Today, parents who suspect that their child has an attention deficit disorder can be more confident that their doctors will know how to diagnose and treat the disorder.

School systems are also beginning to understand more about ADD. Educators are becoming more aware that ADD should not be confused with learning disabilities and emotional disturbances. In distinguishing these disorders in children, school systems are responding to the needs of students with ADD differently than they have in the past. Steps are being taken in schools to provide appropriate educational programs to improve the learning and academic performance of students with ADD at all ages. Teachers and administrators are receiving in-service training about ADD and the federal government has been allocating resources to disseminate information about ADD to schools around the country.

Public awareness is finally catching up with scientific knowledge and parents of children with ADD are hopeful that this will make a meaningful difference in the lives of their children.

What is an Attention Deficit Disorder?

ADD is a neurobiological disorder. It is characterized by attention skills that are developmentally inappropriate, and in some cases impulsivity, and/or hyperactivity.

For quite some time, hyperactivity was considered by many to be the most prominent characteristic of ADD. However, we have come to realize that there are probably different types of attention deficit disorder. Some people with ADD are exceptionally hyperactive and impulsive, others are most notably inattentive, and still others have a combination of all three traits.

These different types of the disorder are described in the Fourth Edition of the Diagnostic and Statistical Manual for Mental Disorders (DSM-IV) which is to be published by the American Psychiatric Association. The three types are:*

- Attention-deficit/Hyperactivity Disorder, Predominantly Inattentive Type;
- Attention-deficit/Hyperactivity Disorder, Predominantly Hyperactive-Impulsive Type; and
- Attention-deficit/Hyperactivity Disorder, Combined Type.

The predominantly hyperactive-impulsive type, along with the combined type, make up the majority of children with attention-deficit/hyperactivity disorder. Probably a third of all children with the disorder are the predominantly inattentive type and do not show signs of impulsivity or hyperactivity. Although attention-deficit/hyperactivity disorder is the technically correct name for the disorder, in keeping with public policy, the term attention deficit disorder (ADD) will be used throughout this book. In specific instances, references will be made to particular types.

In order to qualify for a diagnosis, the individual must have symptoms of inattention, hyperactivity, or impulsivity which are described in the DSM-IV. These symptoms must have been present before age seven. Impairment from the symptoms must be present in two or more settings (i.e., at school, work, and at home). There must be evidence of impairment in social, academic, or occupational functioning. Furthermore, the symptoms must not be the result of another psychiatric disorder.

*DSM-IV Draft Criteria (3/1/93). Copyright 1993 American Psychiatric Association.

Inattention

While attention span is not as visible as hyperactivity or impulsivity, it is usually the symptom of ADD which causes the most problems in school. A child with attention-deficit/hyperactivity disorder, predominantly inattentive type exhibits at least six of the characteristics of inattention described below:

- often fails to give close attention to details or makes careless mistakes in schoolwork, work, or other activities;
- often has difficulty sustaining attention in tasks or during play activities;
- often does not seem to listen when spoken to directly;
- often does not follow through on instructions and fails to finish schoolwork, chores, or duties in the workplace (not due to disobedience or failure to understand instructions);
- often has difficulty organizing tasks and activities
- often avoids, dislikes, or is reluctant to engage in tasks that require sustained mental effort (such as schoolwork or homework)
- often loses things necessary for tasks or activities (e.g., toys, school assignments, pencils, books, or tools)
- is often easily distracted by extraneous stimuli
- is often forgetful in daily activities.

Although frequently inattentive, the child with ADD is not incapable of attending to situations which appeal to his/her interests. They usually have an ample supply of attention when performing highly enjoyable activities, such as playing video games or watching television. In addition, during one-on-one activities, wherein the child with ADD is being closely observed, attention span can be normal.

Hyperactivity-Impulsivity

Although not all children with ADD are hyperactive or impulsive, those who are can't be missed. We're not talking about the typical restlessness or energetic behavior found in most young children. Hyperactive children usually exhibit far greater amounts of restlessness and overactivity, and in many more situations than their non-hyperactive peers. Their impulsivity is reflected in their inability to control their emotions and behavior to a far greater degree than is typical of other children their age.

This is most readily observable in preschool children. A whirling dervish of excitement and energy, the preschool child with ADD can be like a speeding bullet, everywhere at once, and nowhere for very long. They are always touching something, darting about, never satisfied, never sticking with one thing for very long, always curious, and needing supervision. Fortunately, their hyperactivity and impulsivity is at its worst when they are young and they settle down with passing years.

In elementary school, the hyperactive child's activity level slows down from running to restless. They still seem to have a constant source of energy and are ready to start a new activity as soon as they get bored with a previous one. They can be excitable, easily stimulated by their surroundings and are forever wearing out their parents and their friends who need to take breaks once in a while.

The child with attention-deficit/hyperactivity disorder, predominantly hyperactive-impulsive type exhibits at least six of the characteristics described below:

Hyperactivity
- often fidgets with hands or feet or squirms in seat
- often leaves seat in classroom or in other situations in which remaining seated is expected
- often runs around or climbs excessively in situations where it is inappropriate (in adolescents or adults, may be limited to subjective feelings of restlessness)
- often has difficulty playing or engaging in leisure activities quietly
- is often "on the go" or often acts as if "driven by a motor"
- often talks excessively

Impulsivity
- often blurts out answers to questions before questions have been completed
- often has difficulty waiting in lines or awaiting turn in games or group situations
- often interrupts or intrudes on others (e.g., butts into conversations or games)

Prevalence of ADD

It is estimated that ADD affects 3% to 5% of school-aged children within the United States, or approximately two million children. Boys with ADD significantly outnumber girls, in part because ADD in girls is probably under diagnosed. Boys with the disorder tend to be more hyperactive, impulsive and disruptive than girls with ADD and, therefore may be more readily identified.

Related Conditions

Unfortunately, if a child or adolescent has ADD s/he also has a greater likelihood of having other problems with behavior, learning, or social and emotional functioning.

Approximately sixty percent of children with ADD who are primarily hyperactive/impulsive are described by their parents as difficult to manage, strong-willed, stubborn and defiant. They exhibit such unusually high degrees of noncompliance that they are regarded as having an additional disturbance, namely, oppositional-defiant disorder (ODD). Such children or adolescents exhibit many of the following characteristics:

- often lose their temper
- often argue with adults
- often actively defy or refuse adult requests or rules
- often deliberately do things that annoy others
- often blame others for their own mistakes
- are often touchy or easily annoyed by others
- often become angry or resentful
- often are spiteful or vindictive
- often swear or use obscene language

Up to 25% of children with ADD show evidence of a learning disability. A learning disability is a deficit in one or more of the basic psychological processes involved in understanding or in using spoken or written language. These problems are the result of language impairments, perceptual dysfunctions or disturbances in the way information is processed and expressed in written or oral communications. Learning disabled students may show weaknesses in reading, writing, spelling or arithmetic skills. Studies of children with ADD who are primarily inattentive indicate that they are more likely to have language-based learning problems than those with ADD who are primarily impulsive and hyperactive.

Children with ADD may also exhibit a variety of social problems. Energy levels of hyperactive and impulsive children run high and in their play these children can be untiring, zestful, and reckless. Their impulsive nature, short attention span, and abundant energy may cause problems in structured play activities. They can have difficulty in organized sports or other group activities such as drama, arts and crafts, etc.. In activities where concentration is required, turns are taken with other children, and where one is expected to act cooperatively, follow rules, and share ideas and materials problems often occur.

Preschool children with ADD are often excluded from play activities because of aggression. Their low frustration tolerance results in hurting other children when things don't go as they wish and parents of other children tend to find more cooperative playmates. It is not uncommon for elementary school-aged children with ADD to be described as bossy, selfish, and immature in their social interactions. At times they seem to lack a sense of social savior-faire. For this reason they usually find more success in playing with children younger than themselves who more readily accept them. Teens with ADD are sometimes shunned by peers if they display too much reckless, wild behavior.

Children with ADD, predominantly inattentive type, may experience social problems of an entirely different sort. These children are by nature more passive, quiet and noncompetitive than their peers. As compared to their hyperactive counterparts, those who fall into the primarily inattentive type are not impulsive and they tend to be underactive rather than overactive. They are slow in tempo, seem sluggish in their completion of tasks, and may daydream excessively. While they are better accepted by peers than those with ADD who are hyperactive and impulsive, this group of children often remain on the periphery of social relationships. Their quiet nature and somewhat withdrawn personality keep them from taking the initiative to make a lot of friends.

Chapter Two
Causes of
Attention Deficit Disorder

Many theories have been put forth to explain the cause of attention deficit disorder. While most of them have come under scientific scrutiny and have either been accepted as having merit or have been discarded, some continue to receive attention despite the lack of any scientific evidence to support them.

Unproven Theories

The notion that diet is responsible for hyperactive behavior is a good example of an unproven, hard-to-die theory which has caused considerable controversy in recent years. Dr. Benjamin Feingold advocated that artificial flavorings and natural salicylates found in certain foods produced hyperactivity in children. He advised parents to put their hyperactive children on elimination diets to avoid these ingredients. Although a number of parents reported success with such diets, Feingold's theory has not been supported by rigorous scientific investigation.

Dr. Doris Rapp and Dr. Lendon Smith have also written that diet and food allergies play a significant role in causing hyperactivity in children. Despite the wide appeal of their theories, their claims have also received little scientific support.

Effects of fluorescent lighting, misalignment of the spine, candidas yeast infection, and inner ear disorders are other unproven theories which have been put forth to explain the cause of hyperactivity.

Problems related to child rearing practices as a cause of ADD is perhaps the most common and damaging of all the unproven theories about the etiology of ADD. Certainly, methods parents use in raising their child will affect the child's behavior and development to some extent. However, while faulty child rearing practices may contribute to the problems of a child with ADD, there is no scientific evidence to suggest they cause ADD.

Try this question!
(Q) What do diet, food allergies, infections, inner ear disorders, and child rearing practices all have in common?

(A) They don't cause ADD.

Neurobiological Theory

The most widely accepted theory regarding the cause of ADD is that it is an inherited neurobiological disorder. ADD tends to run in families and it is fairly common for children with ADD to have one or more biological relatives with the disorder. Sometimes, parents seeking treatment for their child suspected of having ADD often come to realize that they had similar symptoms when they were children or may continue to exhibit characteristics of ADD as adults.

There is emerging evidence to suggest that children with ADD may have some form of dysfunction occurring in regions of the brain associated with the control and regulation of attention, arousal, and activity. Human and animal studies found that hyperactive symptoms could be modified by chemically causing changes to occur in how transmissions of sensory information are made within the brain. Such sensory information is sent to millions of different nerve cells in the brain, called neurons. This information is sent by neurotransmitter chemicals within the terminals of these neurons. Neurotransmitter chemicals have been found to be directly responsible for behavior, emotion, and cognition in animals and humans. Larger amounts than normal or deficiencies of these neurotransmitter chemicals can have significant disruptive effects on our emotions and behavior. By investigating levels of various neurotransmitter chemicals in the brain (usually through analysis of metabolites of these brain chemicals) some support can be found for an explanation of the cause of attention deficit disorder. Some of the neurochemical transmitters that may be involved are dopamine, norepinephrine, and serotonin. Exactly how any one or all of these neurochemical transmitters affect the development of ADD symptoms is still a mystery.

For the most part, the specific cause of ADD in any one child is often untraceable and unexplained. In a small number of children, brain injury or brain dysfunction may be attributable to a known prior disease or acquired head injury. Some children may have suffered nurological damage as a result of birth injuries associated with difficulties during maternal pregnancy or labor and delivery. Others may have gotten ADD as a result of being born to mothers who abused alcohol or drugs during their pregnancy. However, for most youngsters who display symptoms of attention deficit disorder no evidence of prenatal complications, disease, head injury, or developmental disturbance can be found.

Chapter Three
Diagnosing Children with Attention Deficit Disorder

The primary characteristics of ADD are not difficult to spot in the home or in a classroom. However, not all children who are hyperactive, impulsive, or inattentive have an attention deficit disorder. These same symptoms can be the result of other factors such as frustration with difficult schoolwork, lack of motivation, emotional concerns, or other medical conditions.   In order to make certain that the cause of the child's problems is an attention deficit disorder and not some other condition or circumstance, an assessment is necessary before a diagnosis can be made. A comprehensive assessment of ADD usually requires input from various professionals working together with the child's parents as a team. Members of this assessment team often include physicians, psychologists, and school personnel such as teachers, guidance counselors, or learning specialists.

Although there is no one test that in and of itself is able to validly and reliably diagnose ADD, there are a number of assessment procedures that together can provide useful information in the formulation of a diagnosis. There are significant commonalities in the histories of children with ADD and their families, in the descriptions of these children's behavior on behavior rating scales, the manner in which they perform in school and social settings, and, to some extent, in their performance on specific psychological and educational tests which may lead to an accurate diagnosis.

Early diagnosis of a youngster suspected of having ADD allows parents and teachers to intervene sooner in treating the disorder. Often children as young as four years of age can be accurately diagnosed. In the past, children were less likely to be referred for evaluation until they were older, but with more children attending preschool, those with behavior, adjustment, or possible learning problems are being identified at younger ages. As awareness of ADD increases among doctors, teachers, and parents, more children and adolescents are being evaluated, diagnosed, and treated.

The Physician's Role in the Assessment

The child's primary care doctor, pediatrician, or family physician is often the first person parents turn to for help when there is a medical problem. The doctor is usually familiar with the child's family and medical history and has knowledge of the child through previous treatment contact.

The medical evaluation starts with the physician taking a thorough medical and social history from the parents and child. Findings from this history may alert the doctor as to when symptoms first appeared, in which situations, and to what degree. The doctor will spend considerable time reviewing the child's genetic background, early birth history, and developmental and social history and may ask parents and teachers to complete rating scales to evaluate the child's behavior in different settings. The doctor will also likely perform a routine physical examination. The results of such physical examinations of children suspected of having ADD are often normal, but they are needed to rule out the unlikely possibility of there being another medical illness or related condition which could cause ADD-like symptoms.

Although no specific laboratory test is available to diagnose ADD, the physician may want certain laboratory tests done to determine the overall health of the child. Tests such as chromosome studies, electroencephalograms (EEGs), magnetic resonance imaging (MRI), or computerized axial tomograms (CAT scans) are not used routinely for evaluation of ADD. Such procedures may be necessary when the physical examination of the child, or the medical history, suggests that a genetic syndrome or other health problem could be present.

Additional information about the child may be obtained through consultation with other medical and nonmedical specialists. Psychologists, psychiatrists and neurologists, trained in the assessment and treatment of such neurobiological disorders as ADD, may play an important part in identifying this condition as well as other possible related conditions such as learning disabilities, Tourettes syndrome, pervasive developmental

13

disorder, obsessive compulsive disorder, anxiety disorder, depression or bipolar disorder. Referrals to these specialists can frequently provide vital information to the child's primary care physician regarding diagnosis and treatment.

Remember!
Getting a comprehensive assessment is very important.
Accurate diagnosis will lead to effective treatment of the problem.

The Psychologist's Role in the Assessment

The clinical or school psychologist is trained to administer and interpret psychological and educational tests that can provide important information about the child's intellectual ability, reasoning skills, use of language, perceptual development, impulsiveness, attention span, and emotional functioning. The extent to which such testing is needed depends on the problems that the child is experiencing.

If the background history or school data suggests that the child may have problems with learning, tests to determine the presence of a learning disability may be recommended. The psychologist may administer tests to measure intellectual functioning, academic achievement, and perceptual skills such as visual-motor ability, memory, etc.

For those children who show signs of emotional problems, tests may be administered which are designed to evaluate how the child feels about him/herself and others. Tests to measure self-esteem, depression, anxiety, and family stress are often administered to get some idea of the child's emotional functioning. In addition, the psychologist may ask the parents to fill out questionnaires to better understand how the child reacts in different situations.

Although having been used for over thirty years in laboratories doing research on hyperactive children, computerized assessment devices called continuous performance tests are a relatively new tool in the clinician's arsenal of psychometric instruments for evaluating and treating ADD. By requiring subjects to respond in specific ways to computer generated stimuli, these tests provide information on such sensitive measures as the individual's attention span, reaction time, and impulse control. Comparison of pre- and post-treatment findings help clinicians determine how well interventions such as medications are helping the person with ADD. Some of the more popular computerized continuous performance tests are:

- Gordon Diagnostic System
- Tests of Variables of Attention (T.O.V.A.)
- Conners Continuous Performance Test

In addition to administering tests directly to the child, psychologists collect information by conducting interviews with the child and parents, asking parents and teachers to complete behavior rating scales about the child, and directly observing the child's behavior in the natural environment, i.e., at school or at home.

Behavior rating scales are used by psychologists and others to assess the child's behavior in school and at home. Such scales offer quantifiable, descriptive information about the child, thus providing a means by which to compare the child's behavior to that of others of the same sex and age. Most of the rating scales used to assess ADD provide standardized scores on a number of factors, usually related to attention span, self-control, learning ability, hyperactivity, aggression, social behavior, anxiety, etc.. Some of the more popular rating scales used in the assessment of ADD are:

- Conners Teacher Rating Scale (CTRS)
- Conners Parent Rating Scale (CPRS)
- ADD-H: Comprehensive Teacher Rating Scale
- ADHD Rating Scale
- Child Attention Profile
- Child Behavior Checklist
- Home Situations Questionnaire
- School Situations Questionnaire
- Attention Deficit Disorder Evaluation Scale
- Academic Performance Rating Scale (APRS)

Conducting a psychological evaluation of the child and collecting data from the procedures described above can take several hours to complete. However, the information received from this process is invaluable in helping members of the assessment team arrive at a diagnosis and make recommendations on how to best treat the child.

The School's Role in the Assessment

The school plays a vital role in the assessment of children and teens suspected of having ADD. School personnel can directly observe how the student behaves in a group situation and can compare the student's performance to others of the same age. Schools have access both to current and past information about the student's classroom performance, academic strengths and weaknesses, attention span, and other social, emotional, and behavioral characteristics. School-based behavior rating scales, teacher interviews, review of a student's cumulative records, analysis of test scores, and direct observation of the student in class are typical procedures used to collect data about the student.

School districts around the country are beginning to develop standardized procedures by which to collect information about students who are suspected of having ADD. Many schools utilize a child study team approach to assessment wherein data is collected by team members who then make recommendations to the student's parents and teachers regarding the student's educational needs.

The Parents' Role in the Assessment

The child's parents provide information about the child to other members of the assessment team. Optimally, both parents should be part of the assessment process. Having witnessed the child in a variety of situations throughout their life, parents have a unique perspective on their child's previous development and current adjustment. Information from parents is usually acquired by interview or through questionnaires completed by parents. The focus is usually on obtaining overall family history, current family structure and functioning, and to document important events from the child's medical, developmental, social, and academic history relevant to the assessment of ADD.

The assessment process can be emotionally difficult for both the parents and the child. Parents bring more than just objective information and records to the doctor's office when they proceed with an assessment.

They also bring a mixture of emotions about themselves and their child. For some parents the initial interview with a health-care provider or teacher will be their first attempt at getting help and may be the first time they've ever talked to anyone outside the family about their child's problems. Other parents will be used to discussing these issues, having sought help in the past for their son or daughter. In either case, parents are likely to have been deeply affected by their child's problems and it is not uncommon during the process for many feelings to be expressed.

The Child's Role in the Assessment

An interview with the child offers the clinician an opportunity to observe the child's behavior and can yield valuable information as to the child's social and emotional adjustment, feelings about themselves and others, attitudes about school and other aspects of their life. Information of this sort can be obtained through in-depth interviews with the child and by asking the child to complete psychological tests which evaluate social and emotional adjustment.

Even children with ADD often behave well during such interviews. Therefore, observations of the child's behavior, level of activity, attentiveness, or compliance made during the interview sessions should not be taken as true of the child in other settings. Normal behavior in a one-on-one setting does not diminish the likelihood of the child having an attention deficit disorder.

The Team's Role After the Assessment

Once the assessment is complete, members of the team should communicate with one another to review their findings and come to conclusions with respect to a diagnosis and recommendations. This information may be integrated in one final report, depending on the setting in which the assessment was done, but it is more common for each member of the team to provide a separate report of their findings.

If a diagnosis of ADD (and/or other conditions) is made, a treatment plan will be written in all areas requiring intervention. The physician may determine that medication be prescribed. The psychologist, or other mental health professional, may recommend counseling, behavior modification, or training in social and organizational skills. The school may recommend that accommodations be made by the teacher in the classroom to assist the child with ADD or may make special programs available if the child is deemed to be in need of special education and related services on the basis of a handicapping condition.

If the child is found to have ADD, assessment should not end once the initial evaluation is completed. There should be routine follow-up evaluations by members of the assessment and treatment team to determine how the child is progressing. ADD, being a chronic condition, will often require long-term care and monitoring on a regular basis. Parents will need to coordinate activities of members of the treatment team to work together for the best interests of the child. Coordination of this, whether it be by a parent or a professional, is not easy, but the outcome is usually well worth the effort.

Chapter Four
Treatment of Children
with Attention Deficit Disorder

A multi-modal treatment plan is usually followed for successful treatment of the child or adolescent with ADD. Thus those professionals who played an active part in the assessment may also be involved in the implementation of the treatment plan. The four cornerstones of the treatment plan will likely include medical management, educational planning, behavioral modification, and psychological counseling.

- Medical Management
- Educational Planning
- Behavior Modification
- Psychological Counseling

Medical Management

For many children with ADD the basis of the medical program is management of medication to control symptoms of the disorder. Although most people would prefer alternatives to treatment with medication, the cautious use of certain medications for the child with ADD has been well established as an effective component of the overall treatment plan. Not all children with ADD require medication to manage their behavior, either because their deficits are mild and can be managed by behavior modification strategies, or because their environments both at school and at home are able to be arranged in such a way as to compensate for the child's attentional deficits (i.e., small classes, greater teacher supervision, shortened assignments, etc.). For those children who require the use of medication in treating ADD, the most commonly prescribed classes of medicines are psychostimulants and tricyclic antidepressants.

Psychostimulant Medications

Psychostimulants have been used to treat hyperactivity since 1937 following the first report of the usefulness of Benzedrine for this disorder. Of the psychostimulants, methylphenidate (Ritalin), detroamphetamine (Dexedrine) and pemoline (Cylert) are commonly prescribed. It is suspected that psychostimulants have an effect on the body's neurotransmitter chemicals thus enabling the child to better focus attention, control impulsiveness, regulate motor activity, improve visual-motor coordination, and in general exhibit more purposeful, goal-oriented behavior. Furthermore, when compared to children with ADD who are not treated with medication, those receiving medication generally are less likely to talk excessively in class, blurt out answers to questions, bother other classmates while working, or exhibit aggressive behavior. It is estimated that of those children with ADD who take psychostimulant medication, approximately 70% show improvement.

In general, for the child who is taking Ritalin, the medication's effectiveness can be seen within thirty minutes after ingestion. However, its duration of action is usually only three to five hours, often requiring the child to take a second, and sometimes a third dose, during the day. The starting dose is typically low, usually 5 mg., and is increased periodically by 5 mg. until symptoms targeted for change have improved. Total daily dose typically ranges from 5 mg. to 60 mg. per day.

Even at doses in the lower range some children exhibit what is called a "rebound effect" which can occur a few hours after the last dose of Ritalin was taken. This "rebound effect" is due to withdrawal from the medication and can result in the child temporarily displaying more severe signs of hyperactivity, sensitivity, and irritability than originally seen in the child. While most parents tolerate this rebound of symptoms (it doesn't occur in all children), some find it intolerable and discontinue use of the medication.

A sustained release form of Ritalin (SR-20) is also available. The SR-20 form was thought to be equivalent to a 10 mg. twice daily dose of the standard Ritalin. With the SR-20 Ritalin there may not be as rapid an onset of medication effect as in the standard form, however, the duration of effectiveness on behavior is much longer, approximately seven hours. Studies suggest that the standard form of Ritalin may be more effective than the SR-20 form for some children.

Dexedrine is a psychostimulant which has also been quite effective in the treatment of ADD. Like Ritalin, Dexedrine comes in a short-acting form and long-acting spansules. For children who have trouble swallowing pills, Dexedrine is available as an elixir as well. Considered to be about twice as potent as Ritalin, the typical starting dose of Dexedrine is 2.5-5 mg.. The short-acting Dexedrine works for about 3-4 hours and the spansules probably last about 8 hours. Dexedrine is also given in divided doses, two to three times a day, with a total daily dose range of between 2.5-40 mg. per day.

Cylert, another psychostimulant, has the advantage of a long duration of action (lasting 12-24 hours), but the disadvantage of taking as long as four to six weeks before it reaches its maximum level of effectiveness. Cylert is administered once a day, in the morning, usually at a starting dose of 18.75-37.5 mg. per day with increasing dosage prescribed by the child's physician as needed. Dosage levels of Cylert have not been as well investigated as Ritalin and a total daily dose range of between 18.75-112.5 mg. per day is typical. If a child is taking Cylert, periodic evaluation of liver enzymes is recommended.

The following case history is representative of many cases where medication played a helpful part in the treatment planning for the child with ADD.

Jack, a ten year old fifth grader, was initially referred to his pediatrician for evaluation of academic and behavioral problems in school. Jack's parents provided a history to their doctor which included a consistent record of Jack having difficulty with self-control, attention span, and hyperactivity dating back to preschool. Aside from the fact that Jack had had a fairly good year during parts of third grade (his parents felt his teacher that year was very structured and consistent), he was generally not well adjusted in school in other years.

Parental interview revealed a family history of hyperactivity with both Jack's father and one cousin on the father's side also having similar problems. While the developmental history given by the parents did not reveal any problems with Jack's physical, language, or gross motor development, the behavioral history at home revealed that Jack had difficulty focusing attention on homework (he had no trouble attending to television or video games), was very impatient with regard to waiting his turn in games, was very restless waiting on line or sitting in restaurants, and tended to display impulsive behavior.

Behavioral rating scales completed by both the parents and teacher indicated significantly high levels of hyperactivity and attention span problems. Psychological and educational tests revealed that Jack had high average intellectual ability and was not suffering from any significant emotional problems. While he had adequate achievement skills in the areas of reading, mathematics and written language, he was somewhat weak with respect to perceptual development in the areas of visual-motor ability, short-term memory, and sustained attention. Although he was not weak enough in these perceptual areas to be considered to have a learning disability his weaknesses perceptually, attentionally, and behaviorally had substantially hampered his progress in school over the years.

After thorough medical, psychological and educational evaluations, Jack's pediatrician decided to start him on Ritalin to control symptoms of hyperactivity and inattentiveness. Jack was started on 5 mg. of Ritalin twice a day, morning and noon. A behavior rating scale completed by Jack's teacher at the end of the week was compared to one completed prior to the start of treatment. No significant changes were noted and Jack's medication dose was increased to 10 mg. twice a day. Contact with Jack's teacher a week later revealed improvements in attention span, handwriting, and talkativeness. Jack was still a bit overactive, but his misbehavior was much more easily managed by a behavior therapy program that had also been instituted by his teacher. There were no noticeable side-effects although Jack's parents were alerted to expect signs of appetite suppression and sleep difficulties.

None of these medication side-effects were noted by the parents to any significant degree. Although on a fairly low dose of medication, Jack's symptoms were being effectively treated. Higher doses of medication may have improved his behavior more, but possibly at the expense of class work productivity and learning, so increasing the medication was not indicated. However, after several weeks, Jack's pediatrician prescribed the 20 mg. SR Ritalin so that Jack would only have to take the medication once a day.

Follow-up behavior rating scales sent to Jack's teacher on a monthly basis indicated that Jack's behavior, attention span, and classroom performance had stabilized. Through counseling and attending an ADD support group, Jack's parents had a better idea of what their son's problems were and understood him more. The pressure was reduced for everyone, including Jack, and he and his family got along smoother at home.

As suggested in the case history presented above, there can be side-effects with the use of psychostimulant medications such as Ritalin, Dexedrine, or Cylert. The more common side-effects may include appetite reduction and sleep difficulties and to a substantially lesser degree irritability, nausea, headaches, and constipation. Studies have shown that long term use of Ritalin, two to four years, at doses of 40 mg. per day and more, may effect the child's rate of weight gain and to a very small degree may have a temporary effect on growth. There are no reported changes in the production of human growth hormone (HGH) due to treatment with psychostimulants. Movement disorders such as benign tics or, in more serious cases, Tourette syndrome (a more chronic tic disorder) may appear in a very small percentage of children treated with psychostimulants, but it is unclear whether the use of psychostimulants has anything to do with the appearance of tics. In cases where a tic appears while the child is taking psychostimulant medication the parent should consult the child's physician as it may be advisable to either reduce the dosage or entirely discontinue using the medication.

Tricyclic Antidepressants

Tricyclic antidepressants such as imipramine (Tofranil) and desipramine (Norpramin) have also been prescribed for the treatment of ADD. The bulk of the literature suggests that overall, psychostimulants tend to be superior to the tricyclics in managing ADD symptoms, however, there may be a subgroup of children with ADD, particularly those who show signs of anxiety and depression, who may be better responders to these medications. The effects of Tofranil and Norpramin are long-lasting (usually 12-24 hours) and dosing is usually started in the evening at 10 mg. for children under 50 pounds and at 25 mg. for children over 50 pounds. Larger amounts may be administered in divided doses throughout the day as prescribed by the child's physician. Side-effects with the use of this group of antidepressants includes dry mouth, decreased appetite, headache, stomachache, dizziness, constipation, and mild tachycardia. Doctors may ask for baseline electrocardiograms to be done on the child prior to prescribing these medications since there may be some effect on cardiac conduction.

Other Medications

Clonidine (Catapress) is an antihypertensive medication which has been shown to be helpful for children with ADD who exhibit tics and/or severe hyperactivity or aggression. Clonidine comes in tablet and patch forms. When using the tablet, the physician will typically start with a dose of .025-.05 mg. per day taken in the evening. This can be increased every several days as needed by taking divided doses 3-4 times per day. The clonidine patch offers the advantage of working for several days as medication is gradually released into the bloodstream. The most common side-effect to using clonidine is sleepiness which may be reduced by avoiding a daytime dose initially and giving the medication in the evening. Other side-effects include hypotension, headache, dizziness, stomachache, nausea, dry mouth and localized skin reactions with the patch. Sudden discontinuance of clonidine could result in rebound hypotension.

The Decision to Medicate

Parents of children with ADD must determine for themselves whether they feel comfortable dispensing medication to their child. Most times we take medication to cure a condition. For ADD there is no known medical cure. Like other childhood disorders such as asthma or diabetes, the best that medication can do is to alleviate the core symptoms of the disorder, in this case, impulsivity, inattention, and sometimes, hyperactivity. We aren't even very sure that diminishing these symptoms has any substantial long-term positive effect on learning although common sense suggests, and some studies tend to indicate, that medication may facilitate learning in some indirect way.

If not absolutely for learning enhancement, then what is medication for? Mostly it's for behavior. Behavior in the classroom, behavior in social settings, and behavior at home. Each parent has to decide if behavioral improvement (and the possibility of academic improvement) is enough of an incentive for their child to take medication. We would naturally expect parents to exercise caution in taking this step for their child and we have frequently encountered parents who resisted the idea completely. However, more often than not, we have found that parents using ADD medication with their child were satisfied with the results. In many cases, those parents who showed extreme reluctance at first ended up being in favor of medication usage. However, there are those parents whose experiences with medication have been negative. It is likely that in these cases medication was either ineffective in treating the disorder or their child may have responded to the medication with adverse side-effects.

Medication?
Ritalin
Dexedrine
Cylert
Tofranil
Norpramin
Catapress
Can all help kids with ADD in school and at home!

Parents who are considering the use of medication in treating their child need to make informed decisions and should thoroughly discuss their concerns with their child's doctor. If the decision is to go ahead and give medication a try, then the next questions parents face are: how much, how often, and for how long should medication be used? As discussed earlier, the question of how much medication is needed will depend partly on the child's response to specific doses. There are no variables which we know of to predict optimal dose of any of the medication discussed above. How often medication should be administered (just for school, after school, on weekends as well) will depend on the parents' and treating doctor's goals and objectives in treatment. Some children will need medication throughout the day and evening, and doctors will advocate its use after school and on weekends as well. For others, using medication only during school time will be enough. There is no evidence to indicate that children who take medication seven days a week or during and after school are at greater risk of having health problems than those who take it only on weekdays or during school hours. The question of how long medication should be used through the child's life depends on the types of problems experienced by the child or adolescent as they get older. As you will read later in chapter 7, some children's symptoms diminish as they mature and thus less or no medication may be needed by these children as they get older. For other children with ADD the disorder continues through adolescence and into adulthood. For this group, medication may be useful for many years.

Educational and Behavioral Management

Perhaps the most frequently expressed concern that parents of children with ADD have is with respect to their child's performance at school. Children with ADD often have serious problems in school. Daily reports of poor school performance cause frustration and discouragement for children with ADD and their parents. Typically, teachers describe children with ADD in the following way in school:

- fails to finish what is started
- has a hard time paying attention
- fidgets
- talks excessively and out of turn
- can't seem to stay organized
- can't sit still, restless, or hyperactive
- impulsive or acts without thinking
- often acts before thinking
- daydreams excessively

For quite some time no one seemed to have the answers to help students with ADD in school. Most teachers didn't know what to do with these inattentive, hyperactive children who took up a large part of the day with poor behavior and even poorer work. As a group, teachers received little undergraduate training about ADD and probably had received little, if any, ADD related in-service training during their teaching career. While there are a number of books for teachers on how to manage children with ADD in the classroom, most of these books were published in the past few years and so teachers had few resources to turn to for help. With an average of one to two children with ADD in every class-room and with teachers unaware of how to reach them, these children were in trouble and their parents and teachers knew it.

The reason so few educators knew about ADD was because up until recently ADD was not considered by educators to be a handicapping con-dition in public schools in the United States. No mention of ADD could be found in the Education of the Handicapped Act (EHA; PL 94-142) or in its reauthorized form, the individuals with Disabilities Education Act (IDEA; PL 101-476). ADD was not regarded, in and of itself, as a disabling condi-tion, despite the fact that many children with ADD experienced substan-tial problems in school.

Parent support groups advocated for change of federal law to provide educational services in our nation's schools for children with ADD. As a result, the U.S. Department of Education issued a memorandum in 1991 which directed all state departments of education to recognize the needs of children with ADD in regular and special education. In its memoran-dum, the department encouraged states to abide by the requirements of Section 504 of the Rehabilitation Act of 1973 and the IDEA by taking steps to make certain that children with ADD would receive a free, ap-propriate education. For most children with ADD this could be accom-plished by making accommodations in regular education classrooms to adapt the teacher's teaching style to the student's learning needs. Spe-cial education programs and related services also became available for students with ADD who required more intensive programs than could be provided in the regular classroom.

It is estimated that eighty percent of students with ADD could be taught appropriately in regular education classes as long as teachers are willing to make accommodations in school to meet the child's needs. Ac-commodations refers to adjustments that a teacher makes in the class-room to adapt to the child's unique learning or performance needs. For example, a child with a short attention span may benefit from closer teacher supervision, more frequent positive reinforcement to stay on task, shorter assignments, preferential seating near the teacher, etc.. Organi-zational difficulties may be reduced by assigning a study buddy to help the student with ADD keep track of his/her work in school, teacher initi-ated reminders about work and materials to be brought to and from school, supplying specially marked folders in which to store different kinds of work, etc..

For some children with ADD, behavior modification programs can help the student perform better in school. The purpose of behavior modification is usually to increase the child's on-task behavior, improve compliance to teacher's instructions, reduce excessive talking, improve neatness and organization, encourage completion of classwork, etc.. Behavior modification programs usually involve precise, on-the-spot procedures, incorporated into the classroom by the child's teacher to influence the behavior of the child. Techniques such as positive social reinforcement (a compliment, smile, or other sign of approval), or feedback in the form of a point accrual system or token programs for academic performance have all been successful in improving the classroom behavior and attentional focus of the child with ADD. Response-cost behavior modification programs have also been helpful in reducing negative classroom behavior. In a response-cost system the child receives a "fine" for inappropriate behavior as well as a reward for appropriate behavior. This "fine" may be a loss of points, tokens, play time, etc.. Response-cost programs, coupled with other more positively oriented behavior modification programs, have proven helpful in managing the classroom behavior of children with ADD.

Behavior modification approaches to classroom management usually involve a joint effort between the child's home and school in which several behaviors are targeted for monitoring and change. These may also include: paying attention, completing class work, cooperating with classmates, raising one's hand before speaking, neatness of work, etc.. Usually the teacher monitors specific target behaviors and records the child's performance in some specified way on a card to be reviewed by the parents later in the day. The parents, in turn, provide positive or negative consequences to the child based upon the child's performance for the day or week. For further information refer to the Goal Card Program in Chapter 6.

Behavior modification programs are extremely popular with teachers because of their flexibility, simplicity, and ease of implementation. Generally, such programs can be quite helpful in modifying a child's behavior provided both parents and teacher work together and follow through with the program consistently. A review of the principles of behavior modification and an explanation of specific tools for parents and teachers to use in managing inappropriate behavior are reviewed in later chapters along with other interventions which can assist children and teens with ADD in elementary and secondary school.

Psychological Management

For many children with ADD and their families, psychological counseling is a necessary component of the treatment plan. By the time a child is evaluated and diagnosed it is likely that the family has already gone through considerable stress in trying to cope with the behavioral or learning difficulties that the disorder presents. For most families this stress usually results in confusion and controversy between family members as to how best to deal with the child's behavior. Mothers, who tend to spend more time with the child, are considerably more frustrated in trying to get their child to listen. Hyperactive children are well known to show greater compliance to their father's instructions. Sibling relationships are generally more strained as normal rivalry between siblings is exaggerated due to the impatient, temperamental, and frequent "bossiness" commonly found in the emotional makeup of these children.

Is medication enough?

Using medication alone to treat ADD is rarely enough. Many kids with ADD could benefit from counseling and extra help in school.

Parent education about ADD and related problems is an important part of the counseling process. Parents should make every effort possible to learn about the disorder(s) affecting their child. Understanding usually reduces the frustrations and worries that often dishearten parents. Education about ADD provides parents with the skills they need to become empowered to better help their child. Counselors can educate parents on issues of discipline, parent-child communication, school programming, advocacy, use of medication, etc. Counselors frequently encourage parents to attend support group meetings wherein they could share their experiences in raising a child or teen with ADD with other parents who are going through the same types of problems. At these meetings, parents will find an abundant supply of books, audio and video tapes, conferences, newsletters, and magazine articles available to them and their child. CH.A.D.D., Children and Adults with Attention Deficit Disorders, based in Plantation, Florida, is one such support group. CH.A.D.D. has over 500 chapters nationwide which hold monthly support group meetings to provide information to parents, educators, health-care professionals and adults with ADD.

The hyperactive child also may benefit from supportive counseling to help repair injured self-esteem, overcome feelings of demoralization or depression, to learn more effective problem solving behavior patterns, or to better understand his or her behavior. It is essential that parents and professionals work together in the counseling process to find areas in which the child can excel. Dr. Robert Brooks, a psychologist who studies self-esteem in children, refers to these areas of excellence as a child's "islands of competence" and in his talks and writings he emphasizes the important role that parents, teachers and counselors have in identifying the strengths which a child possesses and building the child's self-esteem on these strengths.

In summary, the treatment of ADD requires multi-modal interventions. Children and adolescents with this disorder will benefit most when parents use a coordinated approach to treatment involving aspects of medical, education, behavioral and psychological disciplines.

Chapter Five
Helpful Tools for
Parents of Children with
Attention Deficit Disorder

Living With a Child Who Has ADD

Most parents of children with ADD face a daily challenge of managing their child's behavior. Interestingly, these parents, as a group, report very similar experiences in raising their children.

Within the home, most children with ADD who are hyperactive have difficulty complying with parental instructions. They frustrate quickly, frequently interrupt conversations, and have a tendency to get into sibling conflicts. Their low frustration tolerance, impulsive response style, and rather demanding attitude can create problems with friends who will regard them as bossy and quick to temper.

Children with ADD who are primarily inattentive and not hyperactive and impulsive drive their parents crazy, not so much by what they do, but more by what they don't do. In this case, parents struggle with unfinished chores, forgotten assignments, slow tempo, and chronic disorganization. They are often described as passive and shy in relationships and may require a steady supply of encouragement to make friends.

ADD tests the limits of most parents' patience and can easily result in marital and family stress. In some families, mothers and fathers report significant differences in their approach to management of their child with ADD, creating tension between parents and confusion for the child. Unfortunately, there are no easy answers to raising these children and no quick-fix methods of child rearing that will consistently be effective in managing their behavior. We do, however, have some useful parenting tips which can help you keep your child on the right track.

Don't get discouraged!
Raising a child with ADD
can be tough. But we do
have some ideas that
can really help.
Know your child's
limits, learn about
behavior modification,
and join an ADD support
group. It's nice to know
you're not alone!

Later on in this chapter we will review the basic principles of behavior modification and discuss specific tools for managing inappropriate behavior. However, it might be interesting to take a moment to look at what research studies have found with respect to parenting behavior in homes of children with ADD.

Several studies of families of such children indicate that these children are notably better behaved when in the company of their fathers as opposed to their mothers. The fact that they behave better for their fathers than for their mothers may be due to the finding that fathers tend to deliver behavioral consequences more immediately to the child and are more punitive in their reactions to inappropriate behavior than mothers tend to be.

Other studies have shown that, in general, parents of children with ADD tend to use more punitive discipline. They yell more, and agree with each other less in how to treat their children than do parents of non-hyperactive children. One might easily draw the conclusion that the parents of children with ADD have poorer parenting skills and that this might contribute to the child's behavioral problems. However, when hyperactive children who were treated with medication displayed better behavior at home and in school, a remarkably positive change was also noticed in their parents' behavior. These parents became less punitive, less coercive, and less negative in their approach to the children. Thus, it is not necessarily poor parenting skills that causes the poor behavior of children with ADD. It is more likely that the childrens' hyperactivity, impulsivity, and inattentiveness bring out the worst in parents.

Before we discuss general principles of behavior modification and review specific parenting skills which may be helpful to you in managing the behavior of your child, it would be helpful to first address the issue of how you are handling the fact that your child has or may have an attention deficit disorder. To relate effectively to a child with ADD, a parent needs to accept the child and his or her problem. Acceptance of the child with ADD refers to the parent's acknowledgment of the disorder and their understanding of the effects that the disorder has on their child's behavior and adjustment at home, in school, and in social settings. Not all parents find it easy to accept the diagnosis of ADD.

Handling the Diagnosis

Parents usually react to the diagnosis of ADD in one of three ways: denial, putting-up-with, or acceptance.

The Parent in Denial

Parents who are in denial generally react to the diagnosis of ADD with doubt, suspicion, and sometimes, anger. They have a hard time accepting the fact that something may be wrong with their child and search for other reasons to explain the child's problems. They may minimize the severity of the problem, "He's just all boy." Or they may attribute the cause of the problem to some outside force not within the child, "It's the school's fault."

The parents who are in denial try to prove to others, as well as to themselves, that there is nothing really wrong with their child. This may create pressure for everyone in the family. Their expectations of the child don't get modified, the disorder doesn't get treated, and the child continues to have problems. Sometimes parents who are in denial put more pressure on the child to do better at home or at school to prove that the child really doesn't have a problem. Unable to live up to a denying parent's increased expectations, the child may become frustrated, angry, and defiant as well as more discouraged, demoralized and anxious resulting in lower self-esteem and usually less appropriate behavior. Parents who are in denial react, in kind, by getting more frustrated, more angry, and less accepting of the child's problem. This vicious cycle of failure and defeat can send the child and the parents spiraling into an abyss of despair.

It takes time for a parent to overcome denial. As with most things in life, we must be emotionally ready before we can take action on issues. Parents in denial should try to keep an open mind about their child's problems. They should read as much information about ADD as they can, attend support group meetings, talk to other parents of children with ADD, and get additional opinions about their child from other experts.

The Putting-Up-With Parent

Putting-up-with parents only semi-accept the diagnosis of ADD in their child. These parents tend to wax and wane between denial and acceptance, unsure and unconvinced in their own mind of the child's ability to control his or her behavior. Putting-up-with parents tolerate the child's inappropriate behavior to a degree, but frequently this tolerance diminishes and the parents temporarily deny the fact that many of the core symptoms of the disorder are just not under the voluntary control of the child. This sometimes leads to aggressive or overly coercive behavior on the part of the parent as well as the parent temporarily underestimating the nature of the attention deficit disorder and ascribing more behavioral self-control to the child than really exists. At such times, outbursts of parental aggression are often followed by guilt with a temporary move in the direction of greater acceptance of the child and his or her problems.

Thus, for putting-up-with parents, the pendulum swings in both directions of denial and acceptance often leading to inconsistent discipline. Putting-up-with parents waver between being afraid to discipline the child too firmly and being afraid to praise the child too freely (because of their uncertainty as to what to really expect from the child). The child frequently becomes confused as to what to expect from the parents and since the parents are insecure in their management of the child, the child will tend to take over more control of the family.

The Accepting Parent

Accepting parents usually greet the diagnosis of ADD with some fear as well as with a sense of relief. These parents, like the other types mentioned above, have always sensed that something was wrong with their child, but they weren't sure what it was. Unlike parents in denial, the diagnosis of ADD for accepting parents takes some of the pressure off. As one parent wrote to us:

"After many, many tests, doctors, teacher conferences, and years of wasted time, and failures and tears, Jeff was finally diagnosed as having an attention deficit disorder. It wasn't easy to find the answer, but the joy we felt in finally having one was overwhelming. Now, we have to deal with the solution."

Accepting parents "deal with the solution" by searching for more information about the disorder. They look for confirming signs of the presence of the disorder in their child and feel hopeful that an accurate diagnosis will lead to effective treatment. Accepting parents think of their child as having a problem rather than thinking of their child as being a problem.

Parental acceptance of the child with ADD avoids a power struggle between parent and child. Instead of gradually becoming enmeshed in an adversarial struggle with the child, accepting parents become the child's advocate. Accepting parents both respect the nature of their child's attentional deficits and associated behavioral difficulties and learn to follow approved treatment plans for the management of the disorder. Accepting parents understand the resiliency of the core symptoms of ADD and are, therefore, better prepared to deal with the ups and downs that their child will go through over the years. Through their acceptance the parents will come to realize that such peaks and valleys are normal and should be expected. Along with the parents' understanding and acceptance of the disorder will come a greater sense of positive regard for the child and for themselves.

Factors Affecting the Behavior of Children

The behavior of a child can be the result of a multitude of factors. Inborn termperament and ability, age and stage of development, values taught by parents, methods of discipline used by parents, and the child's emotional adjustment can play a major role in how s/he behaves and interacts with others. To effectively manage the behavior of a child we must first try to understand the factors that affect him or her and cause the child to behave in the way s/he does.

Inborn Temperament and Ability

Most parents would agree that children are born with their own unique temperament. From the very start, some infants are moody, fussy, strong-willed, and independent, while others display a more agreeable nature as evidenced by smiling, cooing, and allowing their parents to care for them with good humor. Children who exhibit "difficult" temperaments are likely to react more aggressively to frustration, are apt to be contrary, and are more resistant to taking instructions from their parents or teachers. Often, regardless of how much parents try to shape their behavior, these children will continue to be strong-willed. Temperament can be a very resilient trait in a child and can shape the individual's personality for a lifetime.

Obviously, children also vary at birth with respect to ability. Intelligence, eye-hand coordination, memory, social adjustment, alertness, etc. develop differently in children based, in part, on the genes one is born with or other factors related to neurological development. Many children with ADD, for example, are born with a diminished capacity to regulate motor activity, control impulses, and to maintain attention (among other things). Learning disabled children lack age appropriate language and/or perceptual skills, thereby affecting their ability to perform well in school.

The behavior of children may be greatly influenced by factors related to inborn temperament or ability. Children with ADD are a prime example of this.

Age and Stage of Development

Behavior can be explained by the age of the child and the developmental stage the child is going through. All young children are inattentive, impulsive and hyperactive to some degree. These characteristics are a part of their normal development. Youngsters have difficulty focusing attention for a significant amount of time prior to age two and are likely to shift from one activity to another very quickly. We expect them to be impulsive, impatient, and restless. As they grow older, however, their capacity to focus attention and to regulate motor activity should improve.

We expect the toddler who is going through the "terrible twos" to challenge authority as s/he begins to explore the world. We tolerate the young adolescent who is rebelling against parental restrictions in an effort to become more independent and to carve out his/her identity. The particular stage of development a child is in can explain a great deal of his/her behavior.

Parental Values

Children model the values and beliefs of their parents and often express these values and beliefs in their behavior. Parental values provide the foundation for how children learn to interact with others and, perhaps, more than anything else, shapes the child's behavior.

Parents who value honesty, integrity, responsibility, social courtesy, etc. are likely to have children who reflect these values as well. On the other hand, parents who model inappropriate behavior and values will likely find that their children learn from them in the same way.

Behavior Management Style

The style with which parents manage the behavior of their child is closely tied to the values that parents have for themselves and the expectations they have for their child. Some parents expect a great deal from their child and have high expectations. They may choose to manage their child's behavior by setting down firm rules and enforcing them to the letter. Other parents may have a looser style of management, giving their child more leeway in setting expectations and in behavior. In some homes no one seems to be in charge as rules are ambiguous, enforcement is lax, and it seems that the child and parents are on an equal level. To some extent, parenting style will vary with each child in the family as some children need more supervision and management than others.

Parents who themselves are impatient, who overreact, act inconsistently, or who are excessively demanding in their approach to their child may cause misbehavior in their child due to their inability to respond to the child in a more encouraging, positive manner. Overly aggressive or coercive parents may cause their children to react in kind with aggression and noncompliance. Lack of adequate parental attention and supervision of the child, or an overly permissive parental attitude toward child rearing, can give rise to behavioral problems as well.

Understanding appropriate limits and how they should be applied in raising a child is sometimes confusing. Having a child with ADD can confuse the parent even more. It becomes hard to decipher which aspects of the child's behavior are out of his/her range of control and which are purposeful. Parents will react differently depending on how they view misbehavior, i.e., was it intentional or not. Obviously, there are no easy answers here and parents must rely on their knowledge of the child to make the best decisions about discipline.

Stress and Emotional Factors

Our behavior is often closely linked to our emotions. Feelings of well-being, confidence, and happiness are usually associated with positive behavior. Satisfaction with one's self and others brings out the best in children. Unfortunately, dissatisfaction can cause just the opposite behavior. Stress, from one source or another, may trigger anxiety and worry in children which is frequently acted out. Stress in the home, i.e., marital strife between parents, illness in the family, financial worry, and parental depression can significantly affect the way a child behaves.

Common Mistakes in Managing Behavior

To raise a child with ADD successfully requires a great deal of patience and effort. Due to their challenging, and often annoying behavior, children with ADD will test the child rearing skills of the best of parents. Before we go on to discuss some tools for appropriately managing a child's behavior, it may be worthwhile to first review some common mistakes that parents make in discipline.

Failure to provide adequate praise for positive behavior, inconsistency in disciplining negative behavior, poor follow through with limit setting, and disagreement between parents as to what behavior should be disciplined and how are some of the major mistakes parents make in managing the behavior of their child. Remember, a child with an attention deficit disorder, especially one who is hyperactive and impulsive, can bring out the worst in even the best of parents. Look this section over and see if you have made some of these mistakes in the past few days.

Withholding Praise

Common sense tells us that children respond better to praise than they do to punishment or disinterest. Praise motivates children to work harder and to respond in an appropriate way in the future. Unfortunately, some parents make the mistake of withholding praise, thereby, making it difficult for their child to receive enough positive reinforcement and encouragement.

When a behavior is followed by a reinforcer (verbal praise, a smile, a hug, or a reward of some sort) that behavior is strengthened and it is more likely to be repeated in the future. Failure to recognize, praise, or reward the child often enough for doing the right thing is a very common mistake which can lead to a weakening of appropriate behavior. Frequent positive reinforcement is helpful, not only in increasing the probability of a behavior being repeated, but it also helps the child feel good about him or herself, builds confidence, and provides encouragement and motivation.

There are probably several reasons why some parents don't positively reinforce their child's behavior more often. One might be that sometimes a parent may view positive behavior as something that is just expected and, therefore, not deserving of any special recognition or credit. Parents who think that way are more apt to point out when the child is behaving incorrectly and will moreso provide negative attention to those inappropriate behaviors. However, for some children, negative attention may be more rewarding than no attention at all, thus these parents run the risk of inadvertently strengthening the child's misbehavior.

A second reason parents may not positively reinforce appropriate behavior is that sometimes they are fearful of interrupting positive behavior and causing the child to stop what he or she is doing. Parents who do this tend to follow the adage of "let a sleeping dog lie." They remember times when immediately after complimenting the child, s/he exhibited inappropriate behavior, therefore, they try to interrupt the child when s/he is being good as little as possible.

A third reason why parents sometimes withhold praise is due to their disappointment with the child. Parents of children who exhibit high rates of misbehavior often think, "Why should I praise him now, he's been acting like a brat all morning." At these moments parents need to remind themselves that by harboring such negative feelings they may unknowingly create even greater problems by causing the child to become discouraged and disappointed in himself.

Delayed or Inconsistent Discipline

Another common mistake that we make as parents has to do with how quickly and consistently we discipline inappropriate behavior. When an inappropriate behavior is repeated over and over it is possible that the parent has failed to provide swift and consistent discipline. It is a common mistake to avoid actively dealing with our child's problem behavior immediately and consistently. Instead, we often tell the child over and over to stop the misbehavior and threaten them again and again about what will happen to them if they don't stop behaving inappropriately, but all too often we neglect to react to the misbehavior properly by taking the following steps:

    1. issuing a command to stop;
    2. providing a warning to stop; and
    3. giving a punishment if the misbehavior does not stop.

The diagram below depicts proper and improper parental responses to misbehavior.

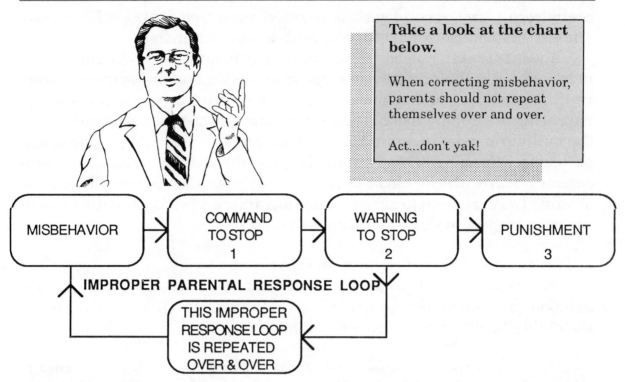

Take a look at the chart below.

When correcting misbehavior, parents should not repeat themselves over and over.

Act...don't yak!

MISBEHAVIOR → COMMAND TO STOP 1 → WARNING TO STOP 2 → PUNISHMENT 3

IMPROPER PARENTAL RESPONSE LOOP

THIS IMPROPER RESPONSE LOOP IS REPEATED OVER & OVER

Punishment is defined as something, generally other than ignoring, which is done to the child and which is directed at weakening the misbehavior. When we neglect to punish inappropriate behavior it gives the child the impression that it is okay to misbehave, that there is nothing wrong with how s/he is acting, and that it may even be fine to act in that way. Frequently, the misbehavior that the child is displaying is reinforcing for the child and so will continue unless stopped. Often ignoring the misbehavior or just telling the child to stop misbehaving and to behave appropriately is not enough to weaken the misbehavior. Parents of any child, and especially of a child with ADD, need to respond to the child's inappropriate behavior **immediately** (within 5 to 10 seconds of giving the order to stop) and need to **consistently** (each and every time the misbehavior is exhibited) provide the child with the appropriate warning to stop and punishment if the misbehavior continues.

There are several reasons why as parents we fail to consequate our child's misbehavior with punishment. Sometimes we don't want to take the time that would be required to carry out the punishment. Sometimes we don't want to go through the "hassle" or the conflict that would result with the child if we were to inflict a punishment. Sometimes we continue to respond to misbehavior by verbally scolding or lecturing the child with the hope that our message will "finally get through." Such verbal tactics usually lead to emotionally intense arguments with the child which generally results in the child getting negative attention for the misbehavior and further deterioration of the parent-child relationship.

A word of caution needs to be mentioned about the use of punishment in managing inappropriate behavior. Excessive use of punishment to correct misbehavior could be more harmful than helpful. Overly aggressive parenting or strongly coercive discipline can result in demoralization and the buildup of resentment in the child leading to additional psychological problems. Punishment, when applied, should be done with reason, consistency, and with the backing of both parents. Positive reinforcement should always be used to acknowledge any improvement the child is making with respect to the specific misbehavior.

Failure to Follow Through on Discipline

Parents frequently make the mistake of responding to inappropriate behavior by threatening to punish at first and then giving in to it when the child's behavior becomes more annoying.

Mrs. Schaeffer, the mother of ten year old Robin, continually gets interrupted by her daughter when she is conducting business on the telephone. She has told Robin over and over again not to disturb her when she is on the telephone, but Robin doesn't seem to remember. Like many parents, Mrs. Schaeffer is unaware of the subtleties of her own behavior and how she responds to Robin when she is interrupted. However, her husband pointed out that his wife's typical response to Robin's telephone interrupting is to first give a reprimand and then to give in, thereby reinforcing the negative behavior:

While still on the telephone mother covers the mouthpiece and responds:
"Robin, I've told you a million times not to interrupt me while I'm on the phone.
Now, what do you want?"

At times we all make the mistake of giving in too often to the child. We can easily fall into the pattern of being a **"NO, NO, NO, NO, YES"** parent. Such parents frequently fall prey to the unrelenting demands and arguments of their youngster. Rather than sticking to his/her decision to allow or not allow a certain behavior the parent breaks down and gives in and the child, therefore, gets reinforced for being demanding and argumentative. The child learns, "If I keep pushing my dad he'll eventually give in." Usually the parent feels "helpless" against the constant demands of the child. If this keeps up the parent may get into a pattern of behavior called "learned helplessness" wherein s/he begins to feel as if nothing can be done to stem the tide of the child's misbehavior so it is easier to give in than to discipline appropriately.

The Villain-Victim-Rescuer Trap

In families where parents frequently disagree on how to manage misbehavior it is easy for the child to manipulate both parents and, in so doing, end up with too much control within the family. In such families a triangle develops making it very difficult to effectively discipline the child. Triangles usually develop when one parent sees the other as being too "hard" or too "easy" on the child. Either parent may react by overcompensating for the other parent's discipline (i.e., My husband says "no" to everything Jennifer asks for, so I feel I have to say "yes" more.).

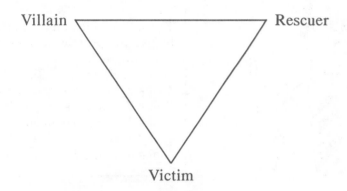

Villain   Rescuer

Victim

In the villain-victim-rescuer trap, the parent who punishes is seen by the child as the villain while the less punitive parent is regarded as the rescuer. These parents are not working together to manage the misbehavior of the child. After one parent punishes, the other parent rescues, thereby cancelling out the effect of the punishment. To make things worse, the child sides with the rescuing parent, sees himself or herself as the victim of the punishing parent, and capitalizes on the support lent by the rescuing parent. The child's behavior doesn't change and the parents end up in arguing with each other.

It is a common mistake for parents not to back each other up enough when disciplining behavior. It is important that if one parent instructs the child to do something and the child hesitates, that the other parent also instructs the child to do as the first parent instructed. By not voicing an opinion, the child will often mistakenly assume that the silent parent supports the child's noncompliance.

Of course, it is not always possible for parents to agree in principle as to whether or not they find the behavior of the child to be objectionable. In such cases, the parents should discuss the issue between themselves and come to a conclusion before instructing the child.

Tools to Manage Behavior

This section describes some useful tools that parents can incorporate in the home to properly manage their child's behavior. After reading about each tool, you are encouraged to complete the worksheet and practice using the tool in everyday situations with your child. These tools were designed to give you some "hands-on" suggestions with respect to child management.

Tools to Manage Behavior.

There are some helpful worksheets to give you practice using the following tools:
Tool # 1: Having the Right Attitude.
Tool # 2: Using Positive Reinforcement
Tool # 3: Using Assertive Communication
Tool # 4: Using Time-Out
Tool # 5: Giving Choices
Tool # 6: Using Token Programs

We suggest you give some serious thought to the behaviors that you would like to modify in yourself as you proceed to apply these tools in your efforts to manage your child. Also, do not try to tackle too much at once in terms of selecting target behaviors to modify in your child. Be specific in your plan. Use the worksheets to help you establish goals for appropriate behavior and work in a systematic fashion to apply principles of reward and punishment.

Tool # 1: Having the Right Attitude

Most parents of children with ADD will tell you that they have "tried everything" in the way of behavioral techniques to manage their children's behavior. Many report that sometimes these techniques work and sometimes they don't. I wouldn't disagree. It is certainly difficult to manage the behavior of a child with ADD, especially if the child's hyperactivity is severe. However, it is not impossible and having the right attitude helps.

First, as we said earlier, it is important to **accept** the fact that your child has ADD. Keep in mind that by accepting the disorder you understand that the core symptoms of impulsivity, inattention, and restless overactivity will **not** be cured by your behavioral interventions. It is likely that the child will still show these symptoms to some degree even though you may have correctly used all the behavior modification tools described in this workbook. Remember, at this point in time, there is no cure for ADD. The best you can do is manage the behavior. So don't feel like you've failed if your behavioral tools work better for you sometimes and not as well at other times.

In raising your child with ADD you will have your emotional highs and lows. During the peak times you will likely feel successful and gratified that your child is doing well at home and at school. During the low times try not to get discouraged. Keep a positive attitude. Remain vigilant in your practice of the behavior modification tools in the following pages. Be consistent, keep your cool, try to figure out what's going wrong, and hang on till better times.

If a highly negative atmosphere has developed in your home as a result of your child's misbehavior it is vitally important that you make every effort possible to establish a positive environment wherein you and your child can interact in a cooperative way. To achieve this, parents may need to overlook certain negative behavior at first and may have to concentrate on positive aspects of their child's behavior. An encouraging, positive attitude on the part of the parent can help set the stage for healthy change on the part of the child.

To take a closer look at your parenting skills please complete worksheet # 1 before reading further.

Worksheet # 1: Common Mistakes In Managing Misbehavior

This worksheet is designed to help parents realize the types of mistakes commonly made in managing a child's misbehavior.

Directions:

Please read each of the following statements about how you generally respond to your child. Put **A** alongside the statement if you **always** act that way, **S** if you **sometimes** do, and **N** if you **never** do.

Mother Father

_____ _____ I tend to scream and yell when my child misbehaves.

_____ _____ I deny my child's requests before hearing them out.

_____ _____ I focus on things my child does wrong rather than right.

_____ _____ I give in to my child's whining or pleading.

_____ _____ If I don't want my child to do something I will tell him/her firmly at first, but I will eventually give in.

_____ _____ I believe parents should disagree in front of their child about discipline if they feel differently from one another.

_____ _____ I tend to repeat instructions to my child too much rather than take action when my child doesn't listen.

If you answered **Always** to most of these questions then take a few minutes and review the section on common mistakes parents make in managing inappropriate behavior. If you answered **Sometimes** to most of these questions don't worry, you're human like the rest of us. If you answered **Never** to all of these questions we offer you our congratulations. You're probably doing a great job of parenting and your child's behavior is probably pretty well under control.

However, if things aren't going so well, try to keep in mind that we all make mistakes. Every parent of a hyperactive child loses their temper, yells when they should be calm, and gives in when they shouldn't, etc.. The tools that follow are easier to read than to apply so don't lose confidence in yourself if you make a mistake. Remember, these are **common** mistakes.

Tool # 2: Using Positive Reinforcement

As we said earlier, the most effective method of managing a child's misbehavior is through the application of positive reinforcement. Behaviors which are followed by positive reinforcement are likely to be strengthened and repeated. Reinforcements can be social (i.e., the close attention of another person, a glance, a hug, a word of approval, etc.) or physical (a gift, a privilege, a token, etc.).

The practice of using positive reinforcement to change the behavior of a child is easy to understand, however, few people do it well. Some parents just find it very hard to give compliments. They withhold their approval, offering praise and congratulations only for outstanding accomplishments. These parents fail to realize the powerful benefits of a few kind words. At the opposite extreme, other parents offer positive reinforcement too freely. They literally gush with praise, hugs, and other displays of affection no matter what the child does. Parents who are interested in changing behavior should provide positive reinforcement immediately after the desired behavior occurs. If and when the child behaves, then reinforce him/her.

Praise and encourage!
Parents who catch their child behaving and praise the child will be ahead of the game in child management.

When teaching a new behavior, it is best to reinforce every time the behavior occurs. New behaviors require immediate and continuous reinforcement in order to get started. For more complicated behaviors it is important to reinforce in small steps. This is called shaping. For example, to shape your child to pay attention to homework it would be important to provide positive reinforcement at several points in the pro-

45

cess of homework completion. Reinforcement could be given for writing the complete homework assignment down in school, for bringing home the proper school books, for getting down to work at the correct time, and while doing the homework. Immediate and continuous reinforcement, delivered frequently and at each small step in the process, is better for strengthening a complex behavior than a parent just complimenting the child once after the behavior is completed.

Physical reinforcers such as privileges, food, refreshments, money, toys, or tokens, etc. are useful in changing behavior. Some parents are hesitant to offer such reinforcers as they feel that they are bribing their child to behave appropriately. Keep in mind that we all work for physical reinforcers (money usually) and that bribes usually refer to payment that one gets for doing something illegal.

Identify areas in which your child excels. These areas of excellence are your child's islands of competence and they can be used to build self-esteem and confidence. An island of competence doesn't have to be anything extravagant, just an area in which your child can be distinguished from other members of the family, i.e., the best dog walker, the funniest joke teller, the video game expert, a real pro at fixing things, etc..

At this time please complete worksheet # 2 on the next page to review the use of positive reinforcement to manage inappropriate behavior.

Find signs of good behavior.

Naturally it feels good to receive a compliment.

Try to give out as many as you can.

Worksheet # 2 : Using Positive Reinforcement

This worksheet is designed to help parents recognize how they have been using positive reinforcement to manage their child's inappropriate behavior and to provide exercises in the delivery of positive reinforcement.

Step 1: Think Positive

List several ways in which you provide positive reinforcement to your child for behaving appropriately. List reinforcers that you think have been most effective in strengthening your child's positive behavior.

Example: Give verbal praise such as, "You're a great listener."

1. _____
2. _____
3. _____
4. _____
5. _____

Step 2: Identify Two Target Behaviors To Reinforce

Fill in the item below with two target behaviors that you would like your child to exhibit more often. Be specific and if the behavior is complicated break it down into smaller parts (as in the example).

Example: Writing homework assignments down in school, getting down to doing homework by self in room, and completing assignments neatly on his/her own.

1. _____
   _____
2. _____
   _____

Step 3: Plan Your Reinforcement

Write down exactly how you plan to reinforce your child each time s/he displays the target behavior listed above.

Every time my child _____ I will reinforce him/her by _____.

Step 4: Reinforce Immediately And Continuously

When strengthening a new behavior it is best at first to reinforce immediately and frequently. That is, reinforce right after you observe the behavior and each and every time the behavior is displayed. Remind yourself to **look for the target behavior** or behavior that resembles the target behavior and immediately deliver the reinforcement. Catch the child being good and focus on the good behavior.

Step 5: Keep Track Of Your Child's Success

Use one of the charts in the back of this workbook (Appendix A) to help your child keep track of his/her success. Fill in the appropriate chart by pasting on stickers, or giving your child points for positive behavior. After your child has filled up the chart provide a backup reinforcer i.e.,

"Mary, after you fill your chart up with stickers for cleaning up your room, we'll go see a movie."

Step 6: Write down two "islands of competence" your child may have.

1. _____

2. _____

Step 7: Think of ways you can expand on these islands of competence to help your child feel good about him/herself?

Tool # 3: Using Assertive Communication

At the risk of oversimplifying, we can break down communication styles of parents three ways:

- Passive communication
- Aggressive communication
- Assertive communication

As you read through the descriptions of each style, try to become aware of how your style of communicating with your child compares to those illustrated below.

Passive Communication

Parents who communicate passively generally put their children's needs and desires ahead of their own. These parents often have difficulty enforcing rules and regulations within their home and may be easily manipulated by their children.

The primary goal of communication by the passive parent is to keep the household environment calm and free of conflict. Frequently, the passive parent is afraid to communicate to the child in an authoritative way for fear of alienating the child and losing love and affection or creating conflict with a spouse. Through passive communication the parent tries to avoid conflict with the child and often rationalizes or minimizes the child's inappropriate behavior in a further attempt to avoid such conflict. Besides having few clear-cut rules in the home these parents' style of communicating their expectations to the child is frequently evasive, weak, and ambiguous.

Example of Passive Communication

Mike is a warm, friendly and likeable person. He is a good-natured father and, like most parents, wants his child, Mary, to have every advantage he can provide. Frequently somewhat insecure about relationships in general, Mike becomes apprehensive in his dealings with his daughter and is somewhat intimidated by her. This significantly affects his management style as follows:

Mike:	Mary, it's time to do your homework.
Mary:	Oh dad, come on! I'll do it after this show.
Mike:	Mary, you know I think we agreed last week that you would do your homework right after dinner.
Mary:	But all the other kids get to watch this show. It's not fair. You're so mean. Can't I watch this one show and then I'll do my homework?
Mike:	Well, okay Mary. I don't feel like arguing any longer. Watch this show, but promise that you'll do your homework right afterwards.
Mary:	I will daddy.

Aggressive Communication

Parents who communicate aggressively generally put their needs ahead of their child's. They tend to enforce rules and regulations around the home in a way which violates the dignity of the child by utilizing threats, harsh punishments, name calling, and other aggressive methods of control.

The primary goal of aggressive communication is domination by power. Aggressive parents typically want things done their way without much regard for the child's desires and they tend to see the nonconforming child as a threat to their power in the family. Winning is generally an important need in the aggressive parent's personality, thereby forcing the child to often be put in the position of loser. The victory for the parent is often achieved, however, through humiliating and belittling with little deference or respect for the child's feelings. Such management tactics, of course, can have detrimental effects on the child's self-esteem and can cause a backlash effect which will result in increased rebelliousness and aggression on the part of the child at a later time.

Example of Aggressive Communication
As a parent, Sue responds to her son in an overly authoritative manner. She deals with Jim in a way which might cause Jim to do what he is told, but probably at the expense of Jim's self-respect and self-esteem.

Sue:	Jim, it's time to do your homework.
Jim:	Oh mom, come on! I'll do it after this show.
Sue:	Jim, you always try to get out of things. You're so irresponsible and lazy. All you ever want to do is play

and sit in front of that television.

Jim: But all the other kids get to watch this show. It's not fair! You're so mean! Can't I watch this one show and then I'll do my homework?

Sue: No. You need all the help you can get in school. I don't know why you put me through this every night. You act so spoiled and rotten. You should be ashamed of yourself. Now, get in your room and don't come out until your homework is done!

Assertive Communication

Parents who communicate assertively stand up for their beliefs and express their ideas and wishes to the child in a clear, direct, reasonable and concerned way.

The primary goal of assertive parents is to provide guidance and structure so that the child can make sound decisions. The assertive parent tends to discourage dependent behavior in the child and, contrary to the aggressive parent, encourages the child to think independently and to act within appropriate limits. Guidelines for behavior are communicated in such a way as to respect the dignity of both parent and child. Assertive communications usually contain clearly defined rules and regulations and assertive parents generally enforce these rules in a firm, yet understanding way. In their management of the child they explain themselves to the child and give the child reasonable opportunity for self-expression as well. The assertive parent, however, remains in charge and in control, not with the intent to dominate or belittle, but with the desire to maintain a leadership role in the home.

Example of Assertive Communication

As a parent, Janet tries to be responsive to her son, David's, behavior while teaching him to be responsible for himself. In doing so, she listens to him with concern, responds in a nonjudgemental way, and helps him make logical and effective choices about his behavior.

Janet: David, it's time to do your homework.

David: Oh mom. Come on! I'll do it after this show.

Janet: David, look at me! Last week we both agreed that you would start your homework after dinner. You decided that you would rather have the free time after school to play and save your homework until after dinner. Isn't that correct?

David: But all the other kids get to watch this show. It's not fair. You're so mean! Can't I watch this one show and then I'll do my homework?

Janet: I'm sorry David. I understand that you are disappointed, but a deal is a deal and you will have to do your homework right now as you promised.

Being an assertive communicator takes time, patience, and self-control. As a parent it is sometimes easier to just ignore your child's misbehavior or to forget about controlling our own tempers. We are all guilty at times of under reacting or overreacting to our children. However, when either of these extremes becomes a pattern in the way we deal with our children serious problems in discipline can result.

Overly passive or aggressive parents must find a balance in the way they manage their child. They should establish rules in the home that are well defined and communicated clearly to the children and should enforce such rules in an assertive, business-like manner with sufficient compassion and understanding of how their child's attention deficit disorder impacts upon behavior.

Complete worksheet # 3 for practice in using assertive communication.

Worksheet # 3: Using Assertive Communication

This worksheet is designed to enable parents to review specific aspects of assertive communication and to practice using assertive commands to manage their child's inappropriate behavior.

Step 1: Distinguishing Between Passive, Aggressive, and Assertive Commands

Mark each item as passive (**P**), aggressive (**AG**), or assertive (**AS**).

1.___ *You never listen. I think you're just lazy. Do your homework.*
2.___ *I think I'd like you to do your homework now. Is that Okay?*
3.___ *You're just a spoiled brat when it comes to being responsible.*
4.___ *Do your homework now if you want to go out and play later!*
5 ___ *Stop fighting with your brother this minute!*
6.___ *How many times do I have to tell you to be good?*
7.___ *You're getting to be such a lazy good-for-nothing*
8.___ *If you misbehave one more time you will go to time-out.*

Statements 1, 3, and 7 are aggressive commands. Statements 2 and 6 are passive commands. Statements 4, 5, and 8 are assertive commands.

Step 2: Characteristics of Assertive Commands

- Say what you mean and mean what you say.
- Give commands politely, yet firmly.
- Make eye contact with the child before a command is issued.
- Follow-through your command with immediate supervision.
- Don't ask the child to follow a command. Remind the child that the command must be followed.
- If the child tries to talk you out of a command, stick to your guns

Step 3: Listening Practice

Listening practice is for children under the age of nine. It is designed to positively reinforce the child for correctly listening to commands. The parent, in turn, gets practice issuing assertive commands as per the rules in step 2 above. When the child complies with the command, the parent positively reinforces the child's behavior. However, if the child refuses to comply, the parent is then to warn the child that s/he will have to go to time-out. Further noncompliance will result in time-out (read the next section on using time-out).

Take five minutes out each day and explain to your child that this time will be used for "listening practice" time and that s/he will get a chance to earn stickers or points for being a good listener (use the sticker chart entitled "All Ears: Being a Good Listener" in Appendix A). Try to make this as enjoyable an experience as possible and introduce this time to the child in a positive way. During listening practice make sure that your child has your undivided attention. Proceed to give several simple assertive commands to the child followed by positive verbal reinforcement for listening and put a sticker on the "All Ears" sticker chart.

For example:
Johnny, please close your bedroom door.
If the child complies, say something like:
You're a good listener. Now, please bring me a pencil.

If the child complies, once again verbally reinforce the child and issue another command. If the child refuses to comply issue a warning that the child will have to go to time-out unless s/he complies. If the child continues not to comply, follow through with time-out. If the child listens to the verbal command, reinforce his compliance and issue another command. Continue until you are finished issuing commands.

Please remember that the purpose of listening practice is to teach your child to follow instructions. Keep these practice sessions positive and fun. Try to make a game out of listening and take a few minutes each day to practice the listening exercise.

Tool # 4: Using Time-out

Time-out is a very effective tool to use in managing inappropriate behavior. Simply put, time-out means that the child is removed from a reinforcing situation and is instructed to spend time in a dull, unpleasant environment. The time-out procedure is a useful tool in producing rapid behavioral change. Some misbehaviors will decrease if the parents ignore the misbehavior. However, for highly annoying misbehaviors such as sibling rivalry, temper tantrums, constant whining and the like, ignoring takes too long to produce behavioral change and it is unlikely that most parents would have the patience to ignore such inappropriate behavior for very long.

The first step in using time-out is to identify those misbehaviors for which you will use a time-out punishment. Use the space in worksheet # 4 to list specific misbehaviors to time-out and alternative appropriate behaviors to reinforce. Remember, whenever you use a punishment program to change misbehavior it is important that you also institute a reinforcement program to encourage more positive behavior. Your Target Behavior List might look something like this.

Misbehaviors to Time-Out	Positive Behaviors to Reinforce
1. Teasing baby sister	1. Playing nicely with sister
2. Temper tantrum	2. Accepts "no" pleasantly
3. Refuses to pick up toys	3. Picks up toys when told to

The second step in using time-out is to decide on a place to put the child when s/he misbehaves. Since time-out, by definition, requires a non-reinforcing environment you should pick a place in the house where there are no toys, games, televisions, books, or people. The child's room is usually not a good place to use for time-out because of all the distractions available to the child. The bathroom is usually a suitable place because it is dull. Some parents prefer to use a time-out chair placed in a corner and instruct the child to sit in the chair facing the wall. The chair should be located in an area of the house which has few if any distractions so as not to inadvertently allow the child to receive any reinforcement while in time-out.

The third step in using time-out is to decide on the appropriate length of the punishment. A good rule of thumb to use is one minute of time-out

55

per year of age of the child for mild misbehavior and two minutes per year of age for more serious misbehavior. It is very helpful to use a portable timer with a bell or buzzer to signal the end of a time-out period.

The fourth step in using time-out involves instructing the child to go to time-out and enforcing the time-out punishment. Since the purpose of using time-out is to replace more aggressive, negative, and/or emotional forms of punishment such as yelling, scolding, and spanking, it is important that instructions to go to time-out be given to the child in an unemotional way using assertive communication. The parent should avoid lecturing, name calling, arguing, or asking rhetorical questions such as "How many times do I have to tell you not to do that?" or "When are you going to listen?" This only serves to provide more attention to the child for his/her misbehavior and may inadvertently reinforce the undesirable behavior.

For example, after observing the child teasing his baby sister the parent should simply say:

"Mark, Stop teasing your sister!"

The parent should then count silently to five. If the child has stopped teasing, the parent should praise him for listening. If the child continues to tease, the parent should walk over to the child, make eye contact, and assertively say:

"Mark, you did not listen to me. If you do that again you will be sent to time-out!"

The parent waits another five seconds. If the child obeys and stops the teasing the parent reinforces the child with appropriate praise for listening. However, if the child continues to misbehave the parent should once again make eye-contact with the child and in a firm, no nonsense voice order the child to go to time-out.

"Mark, you did not listen to me. Go to time-out right now!"

At this point the parent should escort the child to the time-out place, set the timer for the correct number of minutes, and instruct the child to stay there and think about what s/he did wrong until the timer goes off. After completing time-out the child is reminded not to tease his sister again or else he will go to time-out again. In situations where time-out was used because the child did not do something that was asked of him or her (i.e., brushing teeth, picking up toys, etc.) the child is instructed to brush after the time-out period is over. Refusal to do so is followed by another time-out.

Not all children respond to time-out cooperatively. Some children resist going from the start and will aggressively test the limits of the program. Many children do this by arguing with the parent to see if they can successfully persuade the parent not to enforce time-out. Children are quite skilled at doing this and employ all sorts of tactics, such as promising never to misbehave like that again for the rest of their life, blaming their misbehavior on someone else, or just plain denying that they ever misbehaved in the first place. It is essential that the parent ignore these excuses and promises and follow through with time-out regardless of the child's pleadings. By giving in to the child's manipulations the parent loses credibility making it only that much more difficult to enforce time-out with the child in the future.

Some children use more aggressive tactics than just verbal persuasion to avoid going to time-out. In some cases a child will physically resist being placed in time-out. When this happens the parent may have to use physical force to put the child in time-out. The parent could firmly grasp the wrist of the child and walk him or her to time-out or, in some cases, the parent may have to carry the child to time-out. If neither alternative is possible due to the size of the child then the parent may have to remove additional privileges (i.e., television time, play time outside, etc.) from the child until time-out is served.

Another problem may arise once the child is placed in time-out. Some children will tantrum, scream, or threaten to leave time-out prematurely. In such cases the parent must firmly remind the child that time-out will not start until s/he is quiet. If the child continues to misbehave during time-out, do not start the timer until the child quiets down. If the child, nevertheless, terminates time-out without permission the parent should immediately go over to the child and say:

"Time-out is not over! If you come out before the timer goes off I will spank you!" (Parent shows the child that they mean business by speaking in a loud, firm voice).

If the child does not heed the parent's warning to stay in time-out the parent could immediately spank the child (no more than one spank on the buttocks with the parent's hand). Parents who are reluctant to spank their child may further punish by removing additional privileges until the required time-out is fully served. As another alternative, in the case of young children, the parent could hold the child in his/her lap while sitting in the time-out chair. This should be done without speaking to the child or giving the child any attention whatsoever. The purpose of holding is merely to restrain the child in time-out. Usually children dislike being confined in an adult's lap and after a few times of testing the limits the child will respond more willingly to the initial command and go to time-out.

Time-out can be an effective method of punishment for managing misbehavior, however, for it to work it has to be used properly. Please remember, it does take time for the child to realize that mom and dad mean it when they say to go to time-out. Below are some common mistakes parents make in applying time-out:

- not using time-out soon enough after the misbehavior occurs. Most parents mistakenly warn the child to listen or to stop misbehaving several times before issuing a time-out. It is important that you react promptly by using time-out after the first warning to comply.
- letting the child talk them out of using time-out.
- talking too much, arguing, or verbally scolding the child while placing the child in time-out.
- allowing the child to physically intimidate them into not enforcing time-out fully, and
- not using a companion reinforcement program to positively reinforce appropriate behavior.

Remember, disciplining your child takes time and patience. Children with ADD learn to behave best when consequences (both rewards and punishments) are applied immediately and consistently.

At this time please complete worksheet # 4 to review the steps in using time-out and to get more practice in using the time-out tool to correct misbehavior. Keep in mind that it can take anywhere from a few days to a couple of weeks before your child will respond well to time-out. Try not to be discouraged and remain consistent in applying time-out procedures. It might be a good idea **not** to go on to Tool # 5 until you've had a few days practice with using time-out.

Worksheet # 4: Using Time-out

This worksheet is designed to give parents structured practice in using the time-out tool to correct their child's misbehavior.

Step 1: Identify Target Behaviors

Complete the list below with specific **target misbehaviors** that you will consequate with time-out and the opposite **appropriate behaviors** that you will positively reinforce with a specific reinforcer.

Misbehaviors to Time-out:
Example: Interrupting parents during conversation.
1. _____
2. _____

Appropriate Behaviors to Reinforce:
Example: Praise for not interrupting
1. _____
2. _____

Step 2: Choose a Time-out Place

The time-out place will be_____.

Step 3: Decide on the Length of Time-out.

Time-out will last ____ minutes for each of the above misbehaviors.

Step 4: Time-out Enforcement Checklist

- Immediately instruct the child to stop misbehaving.
- Issue a warning to stop or go to time-out.
- Send to time-out if misbehavior does not stop.
- Remain firm and threaten the child with additional punishment if the child refuses to stay in time-out.

Require the child to stay in time-out for the entire length of the time-out (no time off for good behavior, no interruptions for drinks, etc.).

Remind the child after time-out is served that s/he must comply with the original instruction which led to the time-out in the first place.

Backup your spouse with regard to the enforcement of time-out if you are nearby.

Use time-out later on in the day if the misbehavior occurs again.

Positively reinforce the child by praising or rewarding the child for those appropriate behaviors on your target behavior list.

Step 5: Keep Track of the Target Misbehavior

This step requires you to keep track of your progress. For each of the target misbehaviors listed in step 1 record the number of times per day the child exhibited each misbehavior. Remember, the child should receive a time-out **each and every time** s/he does not listen to your instruction first and then your warning to stop the misbehavior. By keeping track of the number of times each misbehavior occurred over a five day period you should be able to determine if time-out is being effective in decreasing the misbehavior.

If time-out has been an effective tool to weaken the misbehavior of the child then you should see the frequency of the misbehavior gradually decrease. If, however, the misbehavior is not decreasing then go over the procedures in step 4 to determine if you are using time-out correctly. If you are and the misbehavior is still not decreasing perhaps one of the other tools for correcting the misbehavior will be more useful.

Time-out Behaviors	Sun.	Mon.	Tue.	Wed.	Thu.	Fri.	Sat.
1._____	___	___	___	___	___	___	___
2._____	___	___	___	___	___	___	___

Tool # 5: Giving Choices To The Child

Children, like anyone else, like to have some control over their environment. We all want to make decisions for ourselves and have some say about what goes on in our lives. Being given the opportunity to make our own decisions is very important, learning to use good judgement in making such decisions is equally essential, and accepting responsibility for the decisions that we make, good or bad, is necessary. The giving choices tool helps us, as parents, to correct misbehavior, but also allows our children to make their own decisions about their behavior and teaches that they must accept responsibility for their choices.

Giving choices to children is an integral part of the child rearing process and involves much more than just correcting misbehavior. It is proper for us to encourage our children to think for themselves and to help them come up with their own solutions to problems in their everyday life. Through actively listening to the child and communicating with the child about events in their life, we, as parents, can guide this decision making process. Parents must also display confidence in their child's ability to reason effectively and to make good decisions on their own. Expressing this confidence provides the child with the satisfaction of knowing that you have faith in them and, of course, contributes positively to the child's self-esteem.

We can extend this philosophy of encouraging the child to think independently and to find their own solutions to problems to the area of correcting misbehavior. The first step in doing this is for the parent to decide whose problem it is that needs to be solved! For example, the child who is happily playing in the family room with every toy he has ever received may be having a wonderful time. He enjoys the fact that not an inch of carpeting can be seen under all his toys and he could not care less that you are expecting guests for dinner in a short time. In this case, who's got the problem? You do of course! Is the child bothered by the clutter of his toys? Does he care whether the family room looks like a tornado came through it? Is he at all concerned about the nervous beads of sweat dripping down your forehead? Of course not! All he's concerned about is having a good time. So, you've got the problem. What do you think is going to happen when you explain your problem to the child?

For example, *"Johnny, we're expecting company for dinner soon. Please clean up your toys so the house looks neat."*

If at this point your child comes to your rescue by cleaning up the toys then your problem is solved. Fortunately, this happens often enough for us to keep our sanity. Unfortunately, it doesn't happen nearly as often as we'd like, especially if your child has ADD. The reason for this is that most children are not interested in solving their parents' problems and are not motivated to take action unless they themselves have a problem. Then we really hear about it!

For example your child might say: *"It's not fair. I never get to do what I want. You're so mean. I don't have to listen to you!"*

After you've decided that it would be fruitless to continue this conversation the second step is to give the problem to the child rather than keep it for yourself. This can easily be done by giving the child a choice.

For example, *"Johnny, look at me! You have a choice! Either you clean this room up right now or you will have to go to time-out ."*

By giving the child a choice between behaving or misbehaving and facing consequences you have shifted the problem over to the child. Now he is faced with the decision to either correct his misbehavior or suffer the consequences.

Suppose the child decides not to correct his misbehavior. It is up to the parent to take the third step and to follow through by enforcing the consequence.

For example, *" It looks like you've decided to go to time-out. Now get in the bathroom and stay there until the timer goes off."*

At this point the parent uses the procedures described in the section describing the use of time-out. There are, however, other consequences which the parent can use in addition to or instead of time-out. Often, child behavioral experts encourage parents to follow through with logical or natural consequences. Logical or natural consequences for misbehavior are consequences which would sensibly or naturally occur within the environment as a result of the child's misbehavior. For instance, it is logical that a child's toys might be taken away for a period of time if the child doesn't clean them up, or for a child who is negligent about doing homework to be restricted from playing until homework is completed, or siblings who are fighting over a toy to not be allowed to play with the toy until they can behave properly.

At this time please complete worksheet # 5 to get more practice in using the giving choices tool to correct misbehavior. This would also be a good time to review worksheet # 6, Selecting Logical and Natural Consequences. This worksheet was designed to assist you in identifying and thinking up logical and natural consequences that can be used to correct common misbehaviors such as: getting ready in the morning, misbehavior at mealtimes, sibling rivalry, misbehavior in the car, misbehavior in public areas such as stores or restaurants, bedtime misbehavior, etc.

Worksheet # 5: Giving Choices

This worksheet is designed to help parents become aware of whether they or their child is having a problem as a result of the child's inappropriate behavior and to review the steps in giving choices to the child, thereby shifting the problem of misbehavior onto the child.

Step 1: Who's Got the Problem?

The list below contains common misbehaviors. If any of them apply to your family put a mark in the column signifying for whom (C for child, P for parent) the misbehavior is usually a problem.

Mark
C or P   **Misbehavior**

_____ 1. Child does not get ready easily in morning.

_____ 2. Child interrupts while you are on the telephone.

_____ 3. Child resists doing homework.

_____ 4. Child won't stay in bedroom at bedtime.

_____ 5. Siblings argue with each other.

_____ 6. Child doesn't behave properly at mealtime.

_____ 7. Child won't get ready for school on time.

_____ 8. Child doesn't keep room neat.

_____ 9. Child doesn't do chores in a timely fashion.

_____ 10. Child doesn't listen when told to behave.

If you marked "C" a lot then you are doing well. This means that when your child misbehaves you are making him or her responsible for the misbehavior. If you marked "P" a lot then you have the problem and may be reacting to it by too much nagging, yelling, or threatening behavior instead of giving the problem back to the child and following through with a consequence.

Remember, children are motivated to solve their problems, but will not likely solve your problems. You must give the problem back to the child.

Step 2: Giving the Problem to the Child

Giving the problem to the child requires you to remain calm and to communicate assertively as you explain to the child his or her choices. Whenever the misbehavior occurs you should assertively tell the child:

"You have a choice. Either you (state the appropriate behavior) *or you will have to* (state the consequence).

Step 3: Following Through

If the child behaves, provide positive verbal reinforcement.

If the child continues to misbehave say:

"It looks like you've decided to _____
so (state the consequence and follow through with it).

When administering the consequence, ignore any arguments the child might attempt to make. Don't respond to verbal comments made by the child and don't lecture, scold, hit, or react in any way other than to enforce the consequence in a calm, business-like way. By remaining calm and unemotional it will help your child accept the consequences of his behavior easier.

After providing the consequence, encourage the child to think about his/her behavior in the future and remind the child that s/he could choose differently next time.

Reward behavior when it's not expected?
    "   " when they are told what
is expected beforehand?

Worksheet # 6: Selecting Logical and Natural Consequences

Time-out is an effective consequence for a good number of misbehaviors. However, at times you may find that logical or natural consequences work as well or better than time-out. Below are some consequences for common misbehaviors and a reminder to positively reinforce appropriate behavior. Write down some other consequences for each misbehavior.

Misbehavior: **Difficulty getting ready in the morning.**
Consequence: As a precaution help the child to choose his/her clothes for the next morning the night before. The next morning wake the child up earlier to allow more time than usual to get ready so that you don't feel rushed. Give the child the choice of either getting ready on time (use a timer to limit the amount of time given to the child to get ready) or s/he will have to go to bed earlier that evening because his/her misbehavior means that s/he must need more sleep. Verbally reinforce or use the sticker chart in Appendix A.
Consequence:

Misbehavior: **Acting up in a store or restaurant**
Consequence: Give the child the choice of either behaving properly or s/he will have to go to the car (or to a time-out spot in the store) if they don't stop because this behavior is not allowed in such places. If the child continues to misbehave then escort the child to the back seat of the car (or to an appropriate pre-selected time-out spot in the store, restaurant, etc.) and stand nearby for a few minutes. If the misbehavior happens again there's not much more you can do at that time, however, the next time you go out, tell the child that s/he cannot go because of their misbehavior last time. Verbally reinforce and use the sticker chart.
Consequence:

Misbehavior: **Misbehaving at mealtime.**
Consequence: If the child starts to misbehave, immediately give him/her the choice of sitting and eating properly or s/he will have to leave the table and go to time-out for several minutes and think about his/her misbehavior (or be excused from the meal entirely). Verbally reinforce or reinforce using the sticker chart.
Consequence:

Misbehavior: **Arguing over a game or toy.**
Consequence: Give the children a choice of playing nicely and taking turns or tell them that you will have to take the game or toy away until they agree to cooperate with one another. Verbally reinforce the children when you witness cooperative play or reinforce with the sticker chart in Appendix A for getting along.
Consequence:

Misbehavior: **Not listening at bedtime.**
Consequence: Give the child the choice to either stay in bed with the bedroom door open or stay in bed with the bedroom door partly closed. If the child opens the partly closed door give the choice of staying in bed with the bedroom only partly closed or with the bedroom door locked (for a few minutes with night light on in room). Usually, at this point, the child will agree to stay in the bedroom with the door open or partly closed. Verbally reinforce the child the next morning for staying in the bedrooom and place a sticker on chart for bedtime behavior.
Consequence:

Misbehavior: **Misbehaving in the car.**
Consequence: Tell the child to stop misbehaving and explain that it's not safe to drive if there is misbehavior. If the child does not listen then pull off the roadway and give the child a choice of either behaving and your continuing to drive or to stay stopped until the misbehavior ends. Occasionally reinforce the child while s/he is behaving properly in the car and use the sticker chart in Appendix A later.
Consequence:

Misbehavior: **Resisting to do homework.**
Consequence: Make sure the child is capable of completing the homework. Set a specific time and place for homework to be started and finished. Offer assistance as needed. Give the child a choice of either finishing his homework **by** the specified time or losing privileges for part of the day. Periodically check on the child while s/he is doing homework and verbally reinforce on-task behavior.
Consequence:

Tool # 6: Using Token Programs

Token programs can be very useful for correcting a child's misbehavior and for encouraging positive behavior. This section explains the use of two types of home token programs ranging from simple sticker chart contracts (to be used along with the giving choices tool) for younger children to a more elaborate home token program for older kids and teens.

Appendix A contains several sticker chart contracts that parents can use with young children to reinforce specific target behaviors that are commonly troublesome for parents. These include: mealtime behavior, getting ready in the morning, proper behavior in the car or in restaurants and stores, cooperative behavior with friends or siblings, and listening to parents. By using the sticker chart contract you can increase the motivation of the child to behave more positively. However, it is important not to try to correct too many behaviors at one time or you'll have a house full of sticker charts and the stickers will quickly lose their value to the child.

You can make the stickers more meaningful to the child by filling out the contract on each sticker chart. In this way the child could exchange earned stickers for a reward after a certain number are collected. However, for displays of misbehavior, as defined by the contract, the child will have to accept the prearranged consequence as well. For your convenience we have partially worded the contracts on each sticker chart.

Sticker Chart Contract

You will get a sticker every time you

_____

However, if you misbehave then_____

_____.

When you get _____ stickers on your chart

you can _____.

For older children, ages nine and up, more sophisticated token programs, such as the home token program, described below, would be more suitable. In this program, points are used to motivate positive behavior. Although they may have some reinforcement value in and of themselves, the points' main value comes from their worth in trade for other reinforcements, i.e., privileges, games, time on the phone, etc.. The first step in setting up a token program with the child is to select several target behaviors which the parent would like the child to exhibit more frequently. Target behaviors should be described clearly and specifically, thereby avoiding confusion and ambiguity. Behavioral descriptions such as, "acts nicely," or "behaves herself" are not specific enough.

The second step in setting up the token program is to make up a reinforcement menu containing items or privileges that the child would want to exchange for points that are earned by displaying the target behaviors. A reasonable rate of exchange is determined by the parents and discussed with the child. After both parent and child have agreed on the behaviors, points, and rewards to be included in the program the chart should be filled in (as in the example below).

The third step in establishing an effective token program is proper enforcement. Points should be awarded immediately after the target behavior is exhibited. If the child does not exhibit the correct behavior on the list, the parents should not lecture or criticize, but should merely point out in a businesslike way that the child will not earn points for that behavior that day.

"You are fighting with your sister so you cannot get points for not fighting today."

Furthermore, it is important that the parent be reasonable in the establishment of a fair rate of exchange of privileges for points. Parents should not permit the child to get an "advance" by borrowing points against the promise of future positive behavior, nor should the child be denied a privilege if his/her points were properly earned. The program should be treated like a contract, with both parties earnestly trying to live up to their respective agreements.

Below is an example of a home token program which is suitable for children age seven and older. There is room for four target behaviors with each behavior assigned a point value. It is advisable when first starting the program with younger children that you start with only one or two behaviors so that the children could get accustomed to the point system and the concept of exchanging points for privileges or rewards from the menu. Additional blank copies of the home token program below can be found in Appendix A.

Sample Home Token Program

Name *Jennifer*   Date *2/8/94*

TARGET BEHAVIORS TO EARN POINTS	POINT VALUE	POINTS EARNED EACH DAY						
		MON	TUE	WED	THU	FRI	SAT	SUN
Does home-work after school	5	5	0	5	5	0	0	0
Make bed and clean room in AM	5	5	5	0	0	5	5	5
Shares and plays nicely with sister	5	5	5	5	5	5	5	5
TOTAL POINTS		15	10	10	10	10	10	10

Menu

Plays game with dad = _10_ Points

Stays up until 8:00 = _15_ Points

Watches up to 2 hrs TV = _15_ Points

The sample home token program on the following page can be used with adolescents. Teenagers on this program have a chance to earn points for target behavior, but they also risk losing points for inappropriate behavior. Additional blank copies of this Home Token Program can be found in Appendix A.

Home Token Program

Name _Jeff_   Date _2/8/94_

TARGET BEHAVIOR TO EARN POINTS	POINT VALUES	POINTS EARNED DAILY						
		MON	TUE	WED	THU	FRI	SAT	SUN
Cleans room	+ 5	5	5	5	0	5	5	5
Homework done after school	+ 5	5	0	5	0	5	0	0
Sets table	+ 5	5	5	5	5	5	5	5
Vacuums house	+ 10	0	10	0	10	0	10	10
TARGET BEHAVIOR TO LOSE POINTS	POINTS LOST EACH DAY							
Fights with brother	- 10	0	-10	0	-10	0	0	0
Uses foul language	- 10	0	0	0	-10	0	0	-10
POINTS EARNED THIS DAY		15	10	15	- 5	15	20	10
BALANCE FROM YESTERDAY		20	20	35	30	45	25	25	5
NEW BALANCE FOR TODAY		35	45	45	40	40	45	15

Extra allowance ($5) = __75__ Points

Movie on Saturday = __40__ Points

Bedtime extended = __15__ Points
_1 hr._

Chapter Six
Helping Children
with Attention Deficit
Disorder Succeed In School

Parents of children with ADD are often very worried about their child's school performance. From preschool through secondary school, teachers frequently describe problems with attention span, distractibility, disruptive behavior, and listening skills as being typical of students with ADD. Characteristics of students with ADD change, however, as the student gets older and the demands of school change.

The Preschool Child with ADD

In most cases, parents of preschoolers are notified pretty quickly when their child is having a problem. Preschoolers with ADD usually have difficulty with self-control and can exhibit such severe hyperactivity and impulsivity that they cannot be easily managed in the preschool classroom. At times, they act out aggressively with other young children as they have trouble sharing and playing cooperatively. Parents of hyperactive preschoolers are not surprised when the teacher calls to ask for help. In all likelihood, as parents they have experienced the same frustrations in raising their child at home as the teacher is finding at school.

Parents and teachers of hyperactive preschoolers have found the typical methods of discipline such as time-out, positive reinforcement, and punishment don't work as well for the hyperactive child as they do for other preschoolers. Successful control over their behavior is hampered by the child's immaturity and lack of internal controls necessary to contain themselves, even with the promise of immediate rewards or threats of punishments. Frequently, parents of hyperactive preschoolers who are also aggressive are asked to withdraw their child from the preschool only to end up in a desperate search for another school that will be able to handle their child's behavior. Such places are rare, and often the parent ends up relying on the good graces of another preschool director or teacher who is willing to give their child a second (or third) chance.

The Elementary School Student with ADD

Most hyperactive children, and those with ADD who are not hyperactive, will be identified as having ADD during the elementary grades. Frequently, kindergarten teachers will report to parents that the child isn't ready to move on to first grade with other members of his/her class. Many will be retained in the primary grade in the hope that they will mature with additional time and be less silly, impulsive, hyperactive, etc.. However, most don't change, even after an additional year, and they continue to have problems throughout elementary school. The course of their problems in school may improve or deteriorate from year to year depending, to some extent, upon a given teacher's instructional style and attitude. However, as demands for academic performance increase with each grade in school the problems of the elementary school-aged child with ADD can multiply.

As the work load increases in school requiring greater concentration, organization, and motivation, symptoms of attention deficit can become more pronounced. This is especially true for those children who have ADD, primarily inattentive type. Since these children are much more quiet than their hyperactive counterparts, they are frequently overlooked in the early years of elementary school as having a problem. They begin to stand out, however, in the intermediate elementary grades as being excessively inattentive, passive, disorganized, etc. In addition to problems with attention span and alertness, students with ADD who are not hyperactive have a greater likelihood of having other learning problems which can affect their ability to acquire skills in reading, mathematics, and written language, signaling the possibility of a learning problem, perhaps a learning disability. Learning disabilities are found in up to 25% of children with ADD (with or without hyperactivity).

For the child with ADD who is unable to attend to a teacher's instructions, getting started on assignments can become difficult and unfinished work can quickly pile up. For those who have problems with organization, finding papers to write on, pencils to write with, or the proper books

73

to use, if, and when, they find the assignment they're supposed to do, can be a complicated task which cannot be taken for granted.

Parents of elementary school-aged children know full well the battles that can ensue over homework. The many steps it takes to do homework (i.e., write the homework assignment down in class, bring the proper books home, settle down after school to concentrate on the work, put the completed homework away in the proper place, remember to bring it to school the next day, retrieve the work and hand it to the teacher) may challenge the organizational and attentional skills of a child with ADD.

In the upper elementary grades, socialization takes on greater importance to the student. Studies of the social behavior of children with ADD, especially those who are hyperactive, indicate that they tend to be disliked by their classmates because their behavior is often bossy, disruptive, and immature. They don't read social cues very well and become overly intrusive with other children, ignoring social conventions such as waiting one's turn, exhibiting modesty about oneself, sharing in an activity, etc.. These are skills that are naturally acquired by other children during elementary school, but are not practiced often enough by children with ADD.

Repeated academic frustration and failure, social rejection, and criticism from teachers and parents throughout the elementary school years can cause the child to develop problems with self-esteem, anxiety, or depression. Frustrated by their lack of success, children with ADD can easily become irritable and sullen and many begin secondary school discouraged and doubtful of themselves.

The Secondary School Student with ADD

Unfortunately, problems associated with ADD don't end when a child becomes an adolescent. Many students with ADD continue to struggle when they get into middle and high school. Although the quality of ADD symptoms changes somewhat during these years, difficulties with attention span, organization and self-control may still persist. Teenagers with ADD often rush through their work, giving far too little consideration for neatness, accuracy, or completeness of assignments in school. Boredom sets in quickly and tasks, which were barely tolerable in earlier grades, become painfully dull and irrelevant in the minds of teenagers with ADD who are interested in more exciting things to do such as dating, driving, etc.

Middle and high school places greater demands on students as they have more teachers to cope with, more work to be responsible for, and more activities to organize. Class schedules can vary from day to day. Long-term projects have to be balanced with short-term assignments in order to get completed on time. Tests are emphasized more and students need to use good study habits to be prepared for class. More reading, note taking, and studying are required to get through textbook chapters with speed, comprehension and adequate recall. Managing these demands requires focus, drive, and persistence, yet for many adolescents, and especially those with ADD, the mood of the moment too often takes precedence over schoolwork.

Teens, who had been diagnosed with ADD when they were younger, often reject the diagnosis when they get into high school. Similar to teenagers with diabetes, asthma, or other chronic health conditions, a sense of invulnerability may develop and they deny being sick or having a problem. Some become more resistant to taking medication to treat their condition and reject help from parents or teachers.

To complicate matters even more, in middle and high school a teacher may be responsible for two hundred or more students and often doesn't have the time to learn about the special needs of individual students. It is easy for a student with ADD to become just another face and for the teacher to be totally unaware why the student is having a problem.

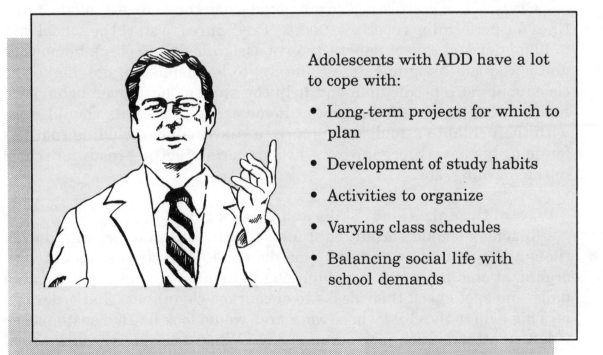

Adolescents with ADD have a lot to cope with:

- Long-term projects for which to plan

- Development of study habits

- Activities to organize

- Varying class schedules

- Balancing social life with school demands

Effective Principles for Teaching Students with ADD

A great deal has been written recently about the types of educational programs that may best serve students with ADD or teacher characteristics which might help children with ADD perform best in school. While no two students with ADD are exactly alike and need precisely the same type of learning environment, there are some general principles which seem to make sense to follow when teaching children with ADD.

Maintain a Structured Classroom

Teachers should strive to maintain structure and routine in their classroom. It makes good sense for the teacher to set well-defined boundaries for the hyperactive child in the classroom and for parents to have similar expectations about behavior in school in place at home.

By having clearly defined classroom rules, teachers communicate their expectations regarding student behavior and performance. However, to be effective, rules must be enforced in a consistent manner. Efforts by the student to obey class rules should be praised by the teacher and a student's success in school should be communicated to the parents at home for additional reinforcement.

Classroom structure is also promoted when there are established routines for performing repetitive tasks. Procedures to start the school day, to hand out and collect papers, to give assignments, to check homework and classroom assignments, to line up, to be dismissed, etc. make the classroom more predictable and help the student form good behavioral habits. Routines are important at home as well. Parents should work with their child to establish appropriate study habits including routines for doing homework, organizing school materials, getting ready for school in the morning, etc.

Train Organizational Skills and Goal Setting

Teachers should encourage students with ADD to be organized even though they may have a hard time doing so. Directing students with organizational problems to straighten up their belongings and work area daily and spot check their desks to encourage cleanliness and order can be a big help to the child whose work area would look like a disaster scene if left unattended for more than a day. When training organizational skills, it is important to have a positive attitude and to adjust your expectations to a level at which the student could experience some success. Look for small signs of improvement in the way the student keeps his/her desk, book bag, etc. and show approval when improvements are made. Frequent positive reinforcement, especially in the beginning, will motivate the student to take more time in managing his work and materials.

Similar guidelines for neatness and organization should be established at home. Teachers should ask parents to cooperate in organization training by spending time with their child to make sure s/he is organized. It would be unfair to expect your son or daughter to keep an orderly desk in school if he is never given the responsibility for a clean room, organized book bag, etc. at home. In addition, parents must be careful that they are good role models of organization themselves. Some children learn disorganization by example.

Students with ADD often have trouble setting goals and carrying out assignments, especially long term projects. Book reports, science projects, term papers, and other multistep, long term projects can present a challenge to the student and a headache to his parents. They will very likely need help from parents and teachers to set realistic goals for completing projects. Breaking projects down into smaller assignments and establishing a time-line for completion of each one will be less threatening to the student and will increase the chances of success at each phase. Teachers and parents should communicate frequently as to how the student is progressing and should provide praise and encouragement freely.

Modify Presentation of Lessons and Assignments

Understanding that students with ADD have difficulty paying attention and lose interest rapidly in tasks, teachers need to make additional effort to modify their instructional style to meet the needs of such students. Before presenting a lesson, the teacher should get the full attention of the class and try to make eye contact with those students who have trouble paying attention. Introducing the lesson in a meaningful way to the student, perhaps by tying the lesson into something of interest to the student, referring to the student by name as the lesson is presented, and offering approval at appropriate times can be a big help.

Teachers should try to gear assignments to the attention span of the student with ADD, not just their ability level. While students with ADD sometimes have trouble getting started on assignments, they almost always have trouble finishing them. Closure is important to all of us and satisfaction comes from a job well done. How good could a child feel about himself if he is always "finishing" his work and trying to catch up to others in class? Teachers can make allowances for the ADD child's short attention span by shortening assignments, giving the child extra time to complete work if necessary, provide breaks within a long work period, or by prompting the ADD child to stay on task.

Parents may find the same strategies work for them at home. If it is difficult for your child to complete homework in one sitting, break it up into smaller bits or time periods and set a timer for work periods. Use incentives, such as earning future play time or television time based upon the amount of work completed or effort sustained.

Use Teacher Attention to Motivate

Teachers should design their classroom and their lesson plans with motivation in mind. Classrooms which have centers of interest filled with ideas to stimulate creative minds and with enthusiastic teachers to keep those minds occupied work best for ADD students. Use the child's personal exeriences during instruction to get the point of lessons across. Find out what interests the student and go from there. Computers can increase motivation and attention to task. Teachers may find that computer assisted learning materials are better able to hold the interest of the ADD student. Colorful graphics, interactive learning, and immediate feedback for responses act like magnets to attract attention. Teachers can also use computer time as a reinforcement for good behavior and work at times during the school day.

Seat Student Close to Teacher

Students with ADD should sit near a good role model or near the teacher so that they can be prompted to stay on task. Try to avoid sitting students with ADD near each other, near windows, by bulletin boards, or close to areas of the room where they are subject to more distractions.

Plan Ahead for Transitions

Students and teachers spend a considerable part of their day in transition. Such times are often difficult for students with ADD due to problems with disorganization and impulsivity. They have trouble settling down and getting their things together to proceed to a new activity. Particularly difficult for these students is the move from an unstructured activity, i.e., physical education, lunch, etc., to a more structured one which requires them to have self-restraint and to work quietly. To assist students with transition the teacher should:

- Establish rules for transitions, i.e., gather the materials you need, move quietly, keep your hands and feet to yourselves, get ready for the next activity.
- Review transition rules with class until routine is established.
- Supervise students closely during transition times.
- Provide immediate and consistent feedback to students doing well.
- Set time limits for transitions, i.e., try to complete a transition within three minutes, etc.

Identify the Student's Strengths

Students with ADD often develop problems with self-esteem as a result of poor performance in school. Teachers can have a powerful impact on the student's perception of himself and as every teacher knows, the building of a positive teacher-student relationship is essential both to facilitate learning and to encourage the development of positive self-esteem in the student. Such a relationship must contain ingredients of caring, understanding, respect, and encouragement. In addition to bolstering shaky self-esteem, a teacher's positive regard will encourage students to put more effort into their work both to satisfy their teacher and themselves.

Teachers should look for areas in which the student with ADD can excel and contribute to others. Such "islands of competence", as referred to earlier, can become a powerful source of pride and responsibility for the student. The student who can think of him or herself as a positive contributor to their class or school is much more likely to develop a positive sense of self than a student who feels s/he has nothing to offer.

Little accomplishments can make a big difference in this area. Find responsibilities that the student can take on and help establish a sense of importance in the student regarding the "work" s/he is doing. Teachers have used this technique for years to help students feel good about themselves. For the student with ADD, who experiences so much criticism, the chance to gain approval can be very meaningful.

Use Effective Commands, Warnings and Consequences to Improve Compliance

Since students with ADD often exhibit higher rates of noncompliance and inattention, it is important that teachers give commands in a way which would increase the likelihood of compliance by the student. Commands which are specific, brief and repeated only once to the child have more likelihood of being obeyed than commands which are: vague (i.e., Do what you're supposed to!); delivered as a question (i.e., Is that what you're supposed to be doing?); too wordy (i.e., If you don't do what you're supposed to do and do you're work you will annoy everyone else and you'll never finish in time for lunch!); or repeated over and over.

Issuing a command alone may not be enough to get a student to do what s/he is told. The command may have to be followed by a warning and a consequence in order for the student to realize the teacher means business. Consequences following noncompliance should be designed to teach the child to comply in the future and need not be overly harsh or punitive. Moderate consequences can have the same effect as severe ones. Loss of a favorite privilege, time-out, additional work, a note to the parents, etc. are all reasonable consequences for most noncompliance. Repeated acts of noncompliance may be handled more effectively with a behavior modification program which will be discussed later. When issuing consequences, teachers should avoid displaying anger or emotion since this may provide some satisfaction to the child resulting in additional negative behavior. Whenever possible, consequences should be delivered in a calm, but firm business-like way.

When working with a student to reduce noncompliant behavior, the teacher should look for signs of cooperative behavior in the student and respond with approval, praise, and occasional tangible reinforcement, i.e., gain of privilege. By increasing the amount of positive attention given to the child, the teacher encourages the student to try harder to comply.

Teach Self-Monitoring

Self-monitoring is a method of teaching students to pay attention to their behavior and to evaluate their own performance leading to better self-control. Self-monitoring requires that the student act as an observer for his or her own behavior and records their observations. Self-monitoring has been used in the classroom to help children pay attention, complete academic assignments, improve speed of classroom performance, control behavior, etc.. This approach is popular with teachers because it is self-administered by the student and takes very little teacher time.

A number of self-monitoring programs have been published to help students with ADD attend better in class. The Listen, Look and Think Program (Parker, 1990) uses an endless cassette tape which beeps every so often to encourage the student to pay attention to assignments. The student marks a form to record whether s/he was paying attention when the beep sounded. Other self-monitoring strategies have been developed to encourage students to work neatly, to use proper social skills with other children, to raise their hands before speaking, etc. The ADAPT Program (Parker, 1992) contains a number of self-monitoring forms to use with elementary school students.

Parents as Advocates

Every parent of a child with ADD should act as an advocate for their child in school. If you don't stand up for your child and make sure that s/he is receiving an appropriate education, then who will? As an advocate you will need to know about the laws which were written to ensure that your child receives a free and appropriate education. You will also need to know how school systems function and what you, as a spokesperson for your child, can do to bring about changes that will benefit your child.

Your Child's Legal Rights

Getting an appropriate education in the U.S. is a right, not a favor. Laws such as the Rehabilitation Act of 1973 and the Individuals with Disabilities Education Act (IDEA), formerly the Education for All Handicapped Children Act of 1975 (EHA), exist in our country to protect those with disabling conditions from discrimination and to improve educational and other services available to them. They ensure that disabled persons, regardless of the nature and severity of their disability, be provided a free appropriate public education and that they be educated with non-disabled students to the maximum extent appropriate to their needs. Furthermore, they stipulate that state and local educational agencies must take steps to identify and locate all unserved disabled children and must evaluate such individuals to avoid inappropriate education stemming from misclassification. The laws also require that procedural safeguards be established to enable parents and guardians to have an active say regarding the evaluation and placement of their children in educational programs.

IDEA and Section 504 guarantee that children with attention deficit disorder have the right to a free appropriate education and that parents have the right to participate in the educational process to make sure their child receives what s/he is entitled. If the educational process fails to work for your child then it is up to you to make sure this guarantee sticks. If you bought a stereo and it didn't work you could use the manufacturer's or seller's product guarantee to take action. You would return with proof of purchase and either get it repaired or replaced or your money refunded. You wouldn't wait for the company to call you to see how you liked their product. You wouldn't sit and complain and do nothing. Not at all. You would take action. It's the same with the guarantee you have on your child's education. If you think your child is not receiving an appropriate education you could use your guarantee (laws) to ensure that the school will find out if there is a problem and to provide the right solution (program or services) for your child. However, it is up to you to make sure that these laws are implemented properly. Your child's school will do some of the work for you, but in the end it is up to parents to monitor their child's educational process. Parents can become good advocates for their child in school if they understand their legal rights and are willing to voice their concerns to the school when the educational process is not working for their child.

Thanks to new changes in policy at the federal level, children with ADD will have a better opportunity to receive a free and appropriate public education. School administrators and teachers are less likely to look at you like you've got rocks in your head when you tell them your child has ADD and needs help. In fact, if your child is exhibiting a problem in school which suggests he may be in need of special education or related services, the school has an obligation to evaluate the child (at no cost to the parent) to determine if s/he is entitled to such services. More and more, schools are the one's identifying this problem and bringing it to the attention of parents. Many school districts offer in-service training on ADD for teachers, guidance personnel, and administrators. No longer does a parent have to feel alone and helpless in securing an appropriate education for their child with ADD.

Nor does the teacher of a child with ADD have to feel as if the total responsibility of ensuring that the child succeeds in school lies with them. Many school districts, aware that the regular education classroom teacher may not have the time or the training to meet the needs of students with ADD, have developed procedures to provide help to the teacher. Such school districts utilize a team approach to finding solutions for students with special needs. Teams are frequently made up of the regular education teacher, a school psychologist or school counselor, and special educator, but can include experts in the area of attention deficit disorder or other disabilities, behavior management specialists, physicians, psychologists, social workers, family counselors, reading specialists, etc. Team members meet to evaluate the student's performance in school and to identify specific educational needs the student may have. The team will then make recommendations to the classroom teacher, other school personnel, and the parent. If the team determines that the student is sufficiently disabled as a result of having an attention deficit disorder, they may write a 504 accommodation plan for the student and instruct the teacher to implement certain accommodations into the classroom to assist the student. Despite their simplicity of use, these accommodations can be very effective in producing desired changes in pupil performance. Usually one of the members of the team is assigned the role of case manager. The case manager has the responsibility of following the student and keeping track of team decisions and the outcome of interventions and procedures used. A list of the accommodations which have been found to be helpful for students with ADD can be found on the following page.

Some students with ADD may need more help in school than could be provided in regular education alone. Such students may be referred by the school team for further assessment to determine if they are in need of special education and related services. Students with ADD may be able to receive such services within the special education category of "other health impairments" solely on the basis of having an attention deficit disorder and are also eligible for special education services if they satisfy the criteria applicable to other disability categories, such as "specific learning disability" or "seriously emotionally disturbed," etc. If so placed, an individualized educational plan (IEP) will be written to meet the student's educational needs.

Effects of Medication On Behavior and Learning

The prescribing of specific medications to assist in managing the behavior and attention span of children with ADD is not uncommon. For many professionals, medical management of attention deficits is an essential part of the treatment plan. As indicated earlier, the use of medications in the treatment of hyperactivity has a long history, dating back almost forty years when Benzedrine was first prescribed to children with attentional problems. Since then, this, and other medications generally classified as psychostimulants, namely, Ritalin, Dexedrine and Cylert, have been found to be quite effective in improving core symptoms in about 70 percent of affected children. Controlled studies of these medications with respect to classroom adjustment indicate that aggressive and purposeless behavior decreases while there is also an increase in goal oriented, on-task classroom behavior. Furthermore, medication can help children with ADD sustain attention longer, reduce impulsivity, improve

ADAPT*

Accommodations Help Students with Attention Deficit Disorders

Children and youth with attention deficit disorder (ADD) often have serious problems in school. Inattention, impulsiveness, hyperactivity, disorganization, and other difficulties can lead to unfinished assignments, careless errors, and behavior which is disruptive to one's self and others. Through the implementation of relatively simple and straightforward accommodations to the classroom environment or teaching style, teachers can adapt to the strengths and weaknesses of students with ADD. Small changes in how a teacher approaches the student with ADD or in what the teacher expects can turn a losing year into a winning one for the child.

Examples of accommodations which teachers can make to adapt to the needs of students with ADD are grouped below according to areas of difficulty.

- seat student in quiet area
- seat student near good role model
- seat student near "study buddy"
- increase distance between desks
- allow extra time to complete assigned work
- shorten assignments or work periods to coincide with span of attention; use timer
- break long assignments into smaller parts so student can see end to work
- assist student in setting short-term goals
- give assignments one at a time to avoid work overload
- require fewer correct responses for grade
- reduce amount of homework
- instruct student in self-monitoring using cueing
- pair written instructions with oral instructions
- provide peer assistance in notetaking
- give clear, concise instructions
- seek to involve student in lesson presentation
- cue student to stay on task, i.e. private signal

This page may be reproduced without permission.

Harvey C. Parker, Ph.D.

*Attention Deficit Accommodation Plan for Teaching

- ignore minor, inappropriate behavior
- increase immediacy of rewards and consequences
- use time-out procedure for misbehavior
- supervise closely during transition times
- use "prudent" reprimands for misbehavior (i.e. avoid lecturing or criticism)
- attend to positive behavior with compliments, etc..
- acknowledge positive behavior of nearby student
- seat student near good role model or near teacher
- set up behavior contract
- instruct student in self-monitoring of behavior, i.e. hand raising, calling out
- call on only when hand is raised in appropriate manner
- praise student when hand raised to answer question

- allow student to stand at times while working
- provide opportunity for "seat breaks" i.e. run errands, etc.
- provide short break between assignments
- supervise closely during transition times
- remind student to check over work product if performance is rushed and careless
- give extra time to complete tasks (especially for students with slow motor tempo)

- provide reassurance and encouragement
- frequently compliment positive behavior and work product
- speak softly in non-threatening manner if student shows nervousness
- review instructions when giving new assignments to make sure student comprehends directions
- look for opportunities for student to display leadership role in class
- conference frequently with parents to learn about student's interests and achievements outside of school
- send positive notes home
- make time to talk alone with student
- encourage social interactions with classmates if student is withdrawn or excessively shy
- reinforce frequently when signs of frustration are noticed
- look for signs of stress build up and provide encouragement or reduced work load to alleviate pressure and avoid temper outburst
- spend more time talking to students who seem pent up or display anger easily
- provide brief training in anger control: encourage student to walk away; use calming strategies; tell nearby adult if getting angry

- if reading is weak: provide additional reading time; use "previewing" strategies; select text with less on a page; shorten amount of required reading; avoid oral reading
- if oral expression is weak: accept all oral responses; substitute display for oral report; encourage student to tell about new ideas or experiences; pick topics easy for student to talk about
- if written language is weak: accept non-written forms for reports (i.e. displays, oral, projects); accept use of typewriter, word processor, tape recorder; do not assign large quantity of written work; test with multiple choice or fill-in questions
- if math is weak: allow use of calculator; use graph paper to space numbers; provide additional math time; provide immediate correctness feedback and instruction via modeling of the correct computational procedure

- ask for parental help in encouraging organization,
- provide organization rules
- encourage student to have notebook with dividers and folders for work
- provide student with homework assignment book
- supervise writing down of homework assignments
- send daily/weekly progress reports home
- regularly check desk and notebook for neatness, encourage neatness rather than penalize sloppiness
- allow student to have extra set of books at home
- give assignments one at a time
- assist student in setting short-term goals
- do not penalize for poor handwriting if visual-motor deficits are present
- encourage learning of keyboarding skills
- allow student to tape record assignments or homework

- praise compliant behavior
- provide immediate feedback
- ignore minor misbehavior
- use teacher attention to reinforce positive behavior
- use "prudent" reprimands for misbehavior (i.e. avoid lecturing or criticism)
- acknowledge positive behavior of nearby student
- supervise student closely during transition times
- seat student near teacher
- set up behavior contract
- implement classroom behavior management system
- instruct student in self-monitoring of behavior

- praise appropriate behavior
- monitor social interactions
- set up social behavior goals with student and implement a reward program
- prompt appropriate social behavior either verbally or with private signal
- encourage cooperative learning tasks with other students
- provide small group social skills training
- praise student frequently
- assign special responsibilities to student in presence of peer group so others observe student in a positive light

short-term memory, and enhance performance on visual-motor tasks.

Numerous studies utilizing rating scales to evaluate the behavior of these children before and during use of medication clearly point out the benefits of medication for children with ADD. Studies of academic performance and dose of medication have shown that at certain doses medication can lead to greater academic productivity in the classroom. Unfortunately, there is not a great deal of evidence to indicate that psychostimulant medications lead to substantially improved performance on achievement tests of spelling, reading, or arithmetic. Thus, learning may not be as positively affected by medication as is behavior and productivity. Improvements in learning may require additional interventions such as remedial teaching or special instruction for some children.

Monitoring Medication

After medication is prescribed, it is important that parents and teachers monitor the child's behavior, mood, and attention span carefully. A child whose medication is insufficient, may continue to exhibit restlessness, inattentiveness and distractibility. Establishing the correct therapeutic dosage of medication is frequently a matter of trial and error, requiring regular feedback by the classroom teacher to the physician. Such feedback may be in the form of subjective teacher impressions, or more objective data may be obtained from the child's teachers through their completion of the Conners' Abbreviated Teacher Rating Scale (ATRS).

As pointed out in Chapter 4, a number of research studies have clearly demonstrated that a curvilinear relationship exists between the dose of psychostimulant medication (i.e., Ritalin) and the completion of academic work in class. This means that as dose increases so does completion of class work up to a point where too large a dose may decrease class work production. Scores on behavior rating scales completed by teachers, on the other hand, continue to improve with increases in medication dosage, however, such improvement should not be at the expense of learning. The ATRS is quite sensitive to medication effects and, therefore, may be used periodically by the child's parents, teachers, and physician to monitor the effects of the medication on classroom performance and behavior.

Below is a sample ATRS completed on James, a nine year old, fourth grade student. The ATRS was completed prior to James receiving any treatment. Follow-up scores on the rating scale, two weeks and four weeks after medication was started, are recorded on the Treatment Evaluation Record presented on the following pages.

Conners' Abbreviated Teacher Rating Scale (ATRS)

Child's Name *James*
Completed on *2/4/94* Teacher *Mrs. Smithson*
Instructions: Please consider the last __/__ (day, week, <u>month</u>) only in filling out the checklist. Check the appropriate box for each item: Not at all, Just a little, Pretty much, or Very much, which best describes your assessment of the child.

Observation	Degree of Activity			
	Not at all	Just a little	Pretty much	Very much
1. Restless or overactive				✓
2. Excitable, impulsive				✓
3. Disturbs other children			✓	
4. Fails to finish things he starts-short attention span				✓
5. Constantly fidgeting				✓
6. Inattentive, easily distracted			✓	
7. Demands must be met immediately-easily frustrated			✓	
8. Cries often and easily			✓	
9. Mood changes quickly and drastically				✓
10. Temper outbursts, explosive, unpredictable behavior			✓	

Comments *James has trouble paying attention. He is talking too much and needs to keep his mind on his work.*

Total Score: *25*

Each item on the ATRS is given a weighting of: 0 for Not at all, 1 for Just a little, 2 for Pretty much, and 3 for Very much. The sum of the points within each column and across all four columns yields a measure of hyperactivity and/or conduct problems. Total scores can range from 0 to 30. In general, children six years old and older who receive scores greater than 15 probably have adjustment problems in class. Such children probably exhibit core symptoms of attentional deficits and hyperactivity which show up as behavioral problems. In general, children with scores greater than 15 who are being treated for ADD may benefit from additional intervention.

Since the ATRS is sensitive to medication and behavior modification effects, it is advisable to establish a baseline level for the child by obtaining teacher ratings prior to the start of medication or behavior therapy treatment. James' score of 25 indicates that he is having significant difficulty in school. Closer analysis of the Very Much checked items indicates that those difficulties center around degree of motor activity, impulsivity, attention span, and mood changes.

Follow-up ratings on the ATRS could be obtained at weekly or bimonthly intervals after the start of medication to assist in determining if the dosage administered is working effectively. The Treatment Evaluation Record can be used by parents and teachers to record ATRS scores on successive ratings by the teacher.

The Teacher Evaluation Record provides the approximate cutoff scores on the ATRS for a sample of boys and girls of various ages. As indicated earlier, scores received at or above the cutoff score should be considered carefully as such scores reflect a higher than desired level of adjustment problems in the classroom as compared to other children of the same sex within that age bracket. In such circumstances, the parent or teacher should communicate with the child's physician to determine whether adjustments in medication type or dosage need to be considered or if other behavioral interventions would be useful to assist the child in making a better adjustment to school.

In the example of James used above, the Conners' Abbreviated Teacher Rating Scale was completed for a second and third time at two week intervals by James' teacher after James started taking Ritalin to control his ADD symptoms. The teacher ratings are reflected in the Treatment Evaluation Record on the following page.

TREATMENT EVALUATION RECORD

CHILD: *James*		AGE: *9*	TEACHER: *Smithson*	
AGE IN YEARS	ATRS CUTOFF SCORES BOYS GIRLS	MEDICATION DOSE & ATRS SCORES		
		DATE: *2/4/94* DOSE: *None*	DATE: *2/18/94* DOSE: *5mg*	DATE: *3/4/94* DOSE: *10mg*
6-8	18 13			
9-11	20 14	*25*	*20*	*10*
12-14	13 7			
15-17	13 16			

Please note medication name and dose in mg.. Note if medication is taken more than once per day and any observable side-effects here:

2/18/94 5 mg twice a day - no side effects
3/4/94 10 mg twice a day - appetite loss - some
sleep problems

Before he started treatment, James' score on the ATRS was above the designated cutoff score for a child his age. Two weeks after he started medication his scores dropped some, but were still higher than desired. Two weeks later, on the third rating of the ATRS, after an increase in medication, James' score remained stable. It is likely that an additional increase in medication dosage is not necessary. Although in this case James' behavior and attention are fairly well controlled, additional learning problems may still exist and periodic parent-teacher conferences or future interventions might be needed.

Refer to Appendix A for blank copies of the ATRS and Treatment Evaluation Record. To determine how your child compares to the average child in his or her age group simply tally up the teacher rating on the ATRS and record your child's score on the correct age line on the evaluation record form. Note the type of treatment, if any, that your child is receiving so that you can make pre- and post-treatment comparisons. If your child's scores are fairly well below the cutoff score for his/her age group then it may be likely that there is no need for treatment or that no changes with respect to any ongoing medication or behavioral therapy would be indicated (if all else is going well, if there are no significant side-effects, and if the child is not overly drowsy or shows signs of not being alert). If, however, the child's score on the ATRS is very near or above the cutoff score for his/her age then this data should be reviewed with the child's physician before making any adjustments with respect to the child's medication or behavioral treatment.

Behavior Modification

Behavior modification programs are frequently used with students who have ADD. The Goal Card, an example of just one such behavioral program, targets five behaviors commonly found to be problematic for children with ADD in the classroom. The Goal Card (I)ntermediate, with five target behaviors, can be effective for children in grades one through eight. For younger children, those in preschool and kindergarten, a more simplified form, the Goal Card (P)rimary, containing three target behaviors is useful.

Below is an example of nine year old James' scores for one week on the Goal Card (I).

Child's Name _James_ Teacher _Mrs Smithson_
Grade _4_ School _Central Elem_ Home Room _206_
Week of _3/7/94_

Goal Card

	MON	TUE	WED	THU	FRI
1. Paid attention in class	3	3	4	4	5
2. Completed work in class	3	2	4	5	5
3. Completed homework	4	4	4	5	N/A
4. Was well behaved	3	3	3	5	5
5. Desk & notebook neat	2	2	4	4	5
Totals	15	14	19	23	25
Teacher's Initials	ms	ms	ms	ms	ms

Rating Scales

N/A = Not Applicable
0 = Losing, Forgetting or Destroying Card

CHECK SCALE TO BE USED
_✓_ _____

1 = Terrible   1 = Poor
2 = Poor   2 = Better
3 = Fair   3 = Good
4 = Good
5 = Excellent

Try For _17_ Points

As you can see in the example above, the five target behaviors on the Goal Card (I) are rated by the teacher each day {children in primary grades (first through second) are rated on the three point scale (1 = Poor, 2 = Improved, 3 = Good) while children in intermediate grades (third through eighth) are rated on the five point scale noted above}. The child is instructed to give the Goal Card to his teacher each day for completion based upon that day's behavior and academic performance. The teacher initials the card and returns it to the student to bring home to his parents for review. Every evening the parents review the total points earned for the day and return the Goal Card to the child for use the following day in school. Encouragement is offered to the child by the parents in the form of verbal praise and tangible rewards (i.e., later bedtime, treats, choice of activity with a parent, etc.) for his or her successes while punishments or fines (earlier bedtime, reduction of allowance, loss of television time) are applied for point totals below a prescribed amount each day. It is important that a combination of rewards and consequences be utilized since children are noted to have a high reinforcement tolerance (meaning that they seem to require larger reinforcers than non-ADD children to encourage similar appropriate responses).

For younger children in preschool and kindergarten, the same procedure will apply with respect to teacher completion of the Goal Card (P) and parent review and follow-up, however, the card is simplified.

CHILD'S NAME _Allison_ TEACHER _Mrs. Wright_

WEEK OF _2/28/94_

GOAL CARD

	MON	TUE	WED	THU	FRI
PAID ATTENTION	2	3	3	2	3
PLAYED NICELY	2	1	3	3	3
FOLLOWED RULES	2	1	3	3	3
TOTAL	6	5	9	8	9

1 = TRY HARDER

2 = BETTER

3 = GREAT JOB

MY GOAL IS TO GET _6_ POINTS

Parents who are interested in using the Goal Card Program with their child will find additional copies of both Goal Card (I) and Goal Card (P) in Appendix A. Be careful to set your reinforcement and punishment cutoff scores at a realistic level so that the child can be successful on the card provided that s/he is making a reasonable effort in school.

Although individual differences need to be considered, we have found that for the Goal Card (I) a score of 10 or more points per day when using the three point rating scales (first or second grade) or a score of 17 points or more per day when using the five point rating scales (second grade through eighth) are effective cutoff scores for starting the program.

For children in preschool or kindergarten who are using the simplified Goal Card (P) a cutoff score of 6 points is suggested for rewards and consequences. Parents of children on Goal Card (P) should be particularly careful to emphasize the reward earning aspect of the program so as not to demoralize the young child if s/he is not being too successful on the program.

As the student using either Goal Card improves in performance, the cutoff score can be raised slightly in accordance with the student's ability. If the child receives less than the cutoff number of points on any given day then a mild punishment (i.e., removal of a privilege, half-hour earlier bed time, etc.) would be provided, however, for points at or above the amount expected a reward (i.e., addition of a privilege, half-hour later bed time, etc.) would be provided. Below is a case study of Jonathon, a nine year old boy, who was treated with behavior modification using the Goal Card (I) program and a five point rating scale.

Jonathon was referred to a psychologist for evaluation and treatment due to a lengthy history of disruptive, noncompliant behavior at school. At the time of the evaluation Jonathon attended a local public school wherein he was in the fourth grade. His last report card reflected average work scholastically, however, his teacher indicated that Jonathon was inattentive, hyperactive and very disorganized in class. Last year's teacher was also contacted and she verified the fact that Jonathon was a "very difficult" child to teach because of his hyperactive and inattentive behavior. Both teachers completed teacher rating scales and rated Jonathon within the range of adjustment problems for a child his age.

Jonathon's parents provided the following birth history. Jonathon was the product of a full term, normal pregnancy and unremarkable delivery. He was born at a weight of 7 lbs. 4 oz. and showed no difficulties with respect to general physical health. Developmental milestones with respect to crawling, walking, and language development were within normal limits. There was excessive restlessness noted from the time Jonathon started to walk and the parents reported an "impatience" in Jonathon and an inability to withstand frustration. He would easily become irritated and upset, often reacting physically and emotionally to requests made of him or if things didn't go his way.

When Jonathon started preschool his teachers reported extremes of misbehavior with hyperactivity and social aggression being at the top of the list. He was asked to leave two preschools because of his aggressive behavior towards other youngsters. His parents were relieved for him to reach the age at which he could enter public school. Unfortunately, his problems didn't improve as he continued to show signs of hyperactivity, defiance, and inattentiveness throughout the next several grades in school.

Psychological evaluation revealed that Jonathon was suffering from a conduct disorder as well as ADD. He was enrolled in individual counseling and a Goal Card program was started to help record his progress in school as well as to make Jonathon responsible for his own behavior.

The Goal Card was explained to Jonathon, his parents, and teacher and everyone agreed to cooperate working with the program. Jonathon was to be rated each day on five target behaviors (see sample Goal Card above) and was to bring the Goal Card home each day for parental review. A cut-off score of 17 was selected as a starting point. Jonathon was instructed that if he earned more than 17 points each day he would be able to stay up until his normal bedtime, nine o'clock. He was told that if he could reach this level for fifteen of the next twenty school days he would earn a present. However, he was warned, if he got less than 17 points on any given day he would have to go to bed a half-hour early.

Jonathon proceeded to test out the program over the next few days. For three days he earned less than the required 17 points and his parents consistently sent him to bed early (even though he missed a soccer practice). Jonathon began to argue with his teacher about the points she gave him in class but his teacher was instructed not to argue back and to remain firm with respect to her awarding points. For the next five days he earned more than 17 points each day. Jonathon's parents complimented him for his fine effort. He continued to do well for the next two weeks and his parents raised the cut-off score to 19 points. Jonathon continued to earn the required number of points each day despite the raised cut-off. His parents periodically reinforced his progress in school and after three months on the Goal Card program Jonathon was doing well enough to use the Goal Card every other week rather than weekly. Within two more months he no longer needed the behavior therapy program.

As with all behavior modification programs consistency is the key to success. Keep in mind that most youngsters will **not** immediately do well on such programs. However, it has been our experience that if parents and teachers remain consistent and steadfast in their utilization of the Goal Card then positive behavioral change generally occurs within two to three weeks. Interestingly, most children who are doing well on the Goal Card are reluctant to stop it because of the positive feelings they derive from being successful in school.

Summary

Students with ADD have unique educational needs which often begin when the child starts preschool and continues on through secondary and post-secondary school. Fortunately, current federal law recognizes that a student may be considered disabled solely on the basis of having an attention deficit disorder and requires that school districts have programs in place for such students to ensure they receive a free, appropriate education.

Most students with ADD could be successfully taught in regular education classrooms with appropriate accommodations made by the teacher. Programs involving medical management and behavior modification can be extremely helpful in enhancing school performance. Some students with ADD may require special education programs and related services.

Chapter Seven
Adults with
Attention Deficit Disorder

Several long term studies which have followed groups of children with ADD through their adolescent years have indicated that some of the core symptoms of the disorder diminish as the child matures. It is generally agreed that with respect to these core symptoms, adolescents with ADD tend to be less active and restless than they were as children. However, as a group, they still tend to display more signs of restlessness, impatience, impulsivity, and concentration difficulties than control groups of adolescents without a diagnosis of ADD.

Unfortunately, despite a decrease in intensity of these core symptoms there is still a tendency for adolescents with ADD to exhibit more discipline problems and to be more rebellious than their non-ADD counterparts. Furthermore, poor school performance, strained peer relationships, and low self-esteem were also found to be characteristic of hyperactive adolescents. Medical management of these children may need to continue throughout adolescence. It was once thought that medication for treatment of hyperactivity should be stopped when the child enters the adolescent years. This is not thought to be the case now.

A number of longitudinal studies have followed hyperactive children through adolescence and into adulthood. Unfortunately, the conclusions of such studies suggest that attention deficit disorder can be pervasive and, in some cases, may have chronic, long-term effects on the individual throughout a lifetime. Although about fifty percent of hyperactive children outgrow the disorder before or during their adolescent years, the other fifty percent, which make up the ADD adult group, continue to be affected to a varying degree throughout their adult lives. A significant number of these adults continue to have problems with concentration, impulsivity, hyperactivity, and organization. They tend, as a group, to have more automobile accidents, to be more geographically mobile, and to exhibit more antisocial behavior. Furthermore, they tend to do less well in school and have less job success than adults without ADD. Self-esteem problems continue to be prevalent along with a higher incidence of overall personality adjustment difficulties.

Several studies have tried to explain why some children with ADD grow up to be better adjusted as adults than do others. These studies have identified several variables that are related to overall outcome with respect to educational, work, emotional, and social adjustment in adulthood. Among those variables which seem to be correlated with positive outcomes in educational attainment and job success are intelligence, family support, and socioeconomic status. General mental health of the individual's family members along with aggressiveness, emotional instability, and frustration tolerance of the child and adolescent with ADD were also important predictors of overall adjustment in adulthood.

Factors that affect outcome in adults.

Factors associated with more positive outcomes of children with ADD as adults are:

• Intellectual ability
• Absence of aggression
• Socioeconomic status of family
• Degree of family support

Adults with ADD, when asked about their experiences during childhood, offer interesting insights into what it was like to have an attentional deficit disorder. Many of their reports focus on the negative aspects of the disorder, particularly with respect to poor social relationships and failure to satisfy others. Frequent reports of family conflict, of not living up to parents' expectations, of social ostracism, of teacher criticism, and of feelings of low self-esteem are heard from adults with ADD who recall their childhood.

While maturation was considered to be important in producing positive behavioral change from childhood to adulthood, a significant number of adults also viewed taking medication as very helpful to somewhat helpful even though many disliked having to take medication as a child. Generally, adults with ADD felt that they also benefited from other intervention strategies such as educational tutoring, family counseling, and individual counseling. In addition to the above interventions, it is obvious that many of these adults highly valued the positive, warm, and close relationships that they were able to develop with family, friends, and significant others as a key factor in their overall adjustment.

Today, more and more adults with ADD are being recognized and diagnosed. Support groups for adults are forming throughout the U.S., thereby enabling adults with ADD to share accounts of their experiences with one another and to learn new ways of coping. Medication treatment, thought at one time to only be useful for children with ADD, is working well for adults also.

Chapter Eight
Explaining Attention
Deficit Disorder to Children

This year, Mrs. Grant's class was chosen to put on the school's Halloween play. Mrs. Grant had been telling her students about the play and everyone in her class was very excited. Every year the children at Maplewood Elementary School looked forward to the Halloween play and each year a different class was selected to perform it. It was a good chance for the students in the play to wear their Halloween costumes and to act out different parts. Also, each year the principal, Mr. Bell, made a special Halloween party and bought a big cake for the class that put on the play.

All the kids in Mrs. Grant's class were busily planning for the play. Mrs. Grant read the script to the class. Mr. Hancock, the school custodian, was setting up special lights on the stage for the play, and even Mrs. Grant's husband was getting involved by building the wood frame for the haunted house in the play. Everything was being planned and rehearsals were going to start in three weeks. The only thing that still needed to be decided was who would get what part in the play.

Jack had never performed in a play before. When he was seven years old he had seen his older sister, Jennifer, play the lead role in her class play. He noticed that everyone clapped and paid a lot of attention to her. Jack secretly wished that he would have a chance to get the lead role this year. He wanted to act the part of the boy who becomes a hero after he rescues all the other children on Halloween night from the wicked witch who lives in the haunted house. Jack often daydreamed of doing brave things like that. When he wasn't daydreaming of one thing he was daydreaming of something else. That was part of his problem.

Jack dreamed of getting the part in the play and being the class hero. However, he knew that he didn't have a good chance of earning the part. Studying for the play and memorizing the lines would take a lot of time and Mrs. Grant was sure to give the part of the boy who saves all the other children to one of the students who always paid attention and did their schoolwork. Jack's problem was that he daydreamed a lot, talked too much to his friends, and hardly ever finished his work in school. That wasn't all. Jack had trouble sitting still. He moved around in

his seat a lot and Mrs. Grant always had to remind him not to tip his chair back because he might fall. Speaking of falling, his pencil did that a lot and so did papers from his desk. He just wasn't able to get organized!

Mrs. Grant seemed to understand Jack. She knew Jack had more trouble than some of the other kids when it came to keeping his mind on his work. She moved his desk closer to her so she could remind him to pay attention. She offered him extra help if he seemed like he needed it. When Jack would talk too much to his friends, Mrs. Grant would encourage him to get back to doing his work. He liked that she did it in a quiet way so that the other kids didn't notice. But most of all, Jack felt that Mrs. Grant really liked him and Jack felt good about that.

Last year, Mrs. Hall wasn't so nice. She would yell at Jack and embarrass him in front of the other kids. Mrs. Hall really got mad when Jack called out answers without raising his hand first or when he talked too much to other students without permission. He just couldn't control himself so well. If he had something to say he just would say it without remembering the class rules to wait his turn. Jack felt that Mrs. Hall always picked on him about his desk being messy and his papers being sloppy. Mrs. Hall called Jack's parents a lot last year to complain about his behavior and Jack would get punished at home for not paying attention in school. Jack's parents were really getting upset. They knew Jack was smart and they couldn't understand why he kept getting into so much trouble at school. Jack couldn't understand it either.

One day, Mrs. Grant gave out the script of the Halloween play to all of the children in her class. She asked them to take it home and read through it. Jack brought the script home but he knew that he would never be picked to play the part he wanted.

That night Jack didn't feel much like eating his dinner. He didn't feel like having any dessert or watching television. Even when his dog, Pepper, jumped up on him to play, Jack didn't pay any attention to him. Jack's mother asked him what was wrong. Jack told her that he wanted to get the part in the play but that there was no use in trying to get it because of his problems in school. His mother told him not to worry and to try to pay more attention in school. She also told him that she would have a conference with Mrs. Grant so that they could all think of a way to help him with his problems.

The next day Mrs. Grant had

98

a conference with Jack and his parents to discuss Jack's problems. Mrs. Grant told his parents that it was a pleasure to have such a fine boy as Jack in her class. She also said that she realized that Jack had a problem with paying attention, completing all his work in class, sitting still, and keeping his desk and work neat. She went on to tell Jack's parents that she knew of other students who had the same problems. Mrs. Grant asked Jack and his parents if they would like to all work together on a plan to help Jack do better in school. They all agreed that

they would like to help in any way they could. Mrs. Grant told Jack that she would remind him to pay attention, to sit still, to finish his work, and to be neat. Each day, she said, she would fill out a Goal Card. She would give him points on the card so Jack and his parents would know how he was doing in school every day. Jack agreed to take the card home to his parents after school each day and return it to school the next morning.

Mrs. Grant filled out Jack's Goal card every day and gave him points for his work in school If he had a good day and earned a lot of points then his parents would reward him in some way, but if he had a bad day and didn't earn many points he would miss the reward and he might even have to miss some television that night or go to bed a little early.

For the next few days Jack really tried hard to follow the plan in school. Whenever he forgot to pay attention his teacher would just go over to his desk and gently remind him to keep his mind on his work. Every day after Mrs. Grant filled out the Goal Card, Jack would bring it home for his parents to look at. After a while, everybody noticed that Jack was earning more and more points each day and that he was doing better in school. He paid attention better, he completed his work in class, he sat still longer, and his work got neater and neater. Jack also got happier and happier. Each day he earned a lot of points and he felt better about himself. When Mrs. Grant asked each of the children what part they would like to have in the Halloween play, Jack raised his hand and told her that he would like to play the part of the boy who saved all of the children in the haunted house. Mrs. Grant said that since Jack had been improving so much in school he could have the part. All the kids in the class agreed that Jack really had earned the part.

On the day of the Halloween play, Jack was nervous but also very excited. His parents and his sister, Jennifer, had come to watch him perform. After the play was over, everyone applauded and Jack got a standing ovation from the audience and the other students. Jack was proud of himself and so were his parents and his sister. The next day, Jack and his classmates celebrated when Mr. Bell brought a big cake to Mrs. Grant's classroom for the party.

Books and Videos to Help Children Understand Attention Deficit Disorder

A number of books and videos have been published to help children and adolescents with ADD to better understand themselves and others. The following books and videos will be helpful in assisting parents and teachers who would like to acquaint children about ADD. These materials can be ordered directly from their publishers (see suggested reading section) or from the A.D.D. WareHouse, (800) 233-9273.

Shelley, The Hyperactive Turtle
Deborah Moss
Shelley moves like a rocket and is unable to sit still for even the shortest periods of time. Because he and the other turtles are unable to understand why he is so wiggly and squirmy, Shelley begins to feel out-of-place. But after a visit to the doctor, Shelley learns what "hyperactive" means and gets the right kind of help. Ages 3-7.

Otto Leans About His Medication
Mathew Galvin, M.D.
Dr. Galvin wrote a wonderful book explaining attention deficit disorder in story format. It is intended to be read to and by the child. Otto, a fidgety young car that has trouble paying attention in school, visits a special mechanic who prescribes a medicine to control his hyperactive behavior. Ages 5-10.

Eagle Eyes:
A Child's View of Attention Deficit Disorder
Jeanne Gehret, M.A.
Clumsy and impulsive on a nature walk, Ben drives away the birds he admires. Over time, however, he learns to focus his attention like an eagle on the things that really count. By the end of this sympathetic story, Ben successfully helps his father when an emergency arises. *Eagle Eyes* helps readers of all ages understand ADD and gives practical suggestions for organization, social cues and self-calming. Expressive illustrations with a nature theme enhance this tale for reluctant readers. Ages 6-12.

Learning To Slow Down and Pay Attention
Kathleen Nadeau, Ph.D. and Ellen Dixon, Ph.D.
Written for children to read, and illustrated with delightful cartoons and activity pages to engage the child's interest. *Learning To Slow Down and Pay Attention* helps children to identify problems and explains how their parents, their doctor and their teacher can help. In an easy-to-understand language the book describes how an ADD child can learn to pay better attention in class, manage feelings, get more organized, and learn to problem solve. Ages 6-14.

Jumpin' Johnny Get Back To Work!
A Child's Guide to ADHD/Hyperactivity
Michael Gordon, Ph.D.
This entertaining and informative book and video will help children understand the essential concepts involved in the evaluation and treatment of ADHD. *Jumpin' Johnny* tells what it's like to be inattentive and impulsive, and how his family and school work with him to make life easier. Children find this book to be amusing, educational and accurate in its depiction of the challenges that confront them daily. Dr. Gordon's humor and extensive clinical experience with ADHD children shine through every page of this charming but realistic story. Ages 6-11.

Making the Grade:
An Adolescent's Struggle with ADD
Roberta N. Parker
Making the Grade is the heartwarming story of seventh grader Jim Jerome's struggle to succeed in school. Eager to make a good showing in junior high, Jim soon finds his problems with self-control and inattention threaten his chances of success scholastically and athletically. With the help of his parents, teachers and concerned health care professionals, Jim learns about ADD and ways to help himself.

Although a fictional account of how ADD can affect pre-teen and young teenage students, *Making the Grade* is, nonetheless, a very relatable story for nine to fourteen year old adolescents who have attention deficit disorder. Following the story is a section entitled Facts About ADD: Commonly Asked Questions which offers more direct information to young readers. Dr. Harvey Parker explains the symptoms, causes, treatments and outcomes of ADD in a frank and positive way.

Slam Dunk:
A Young Boy's Struggle with ADD
Roberta N. Parker

Toby Butler is an inner city, fifth-grade student with a love of basketball and a problem paying attention. He's diagnosed with ADD which has affected his home and school life. Use of classroom accommodations are discussed and behavioral and medical interventions are described so that children can understand them. Ages 8-12.

Putting On the Brakes
Patricia O. Quinn, M.D. and Judith Stern, M.A.

An honest, accessible overview of attention deficit hyperactivity disorder for children ages 8 to 12. Written for children to read, *Putting On The Brakes* focuses on the feelings and emotions of children with ADD and suggests specific techniques for gaining control of the situation, becoming better organized, and functioning better at school, home, and with friends. Children with ADD will find the acknowledgment and explanation of their problems a relief, and the coping strategies a great help. The book addresses such topics as the physiology and symptoms of ADD, medication used in treatment, and various types of family and community support that are available.

Keeping A Head In School: A Student's Book About Learning Abilities and Learning Disorders
Mel Levine, M.D.

This book, written especially for students by Dr. Mel Levine, a pediatrician and well known authority on learning problems, demystifies learning disorders for young people affected by them. *Keeping A Head In School,* helps nine to fifteen year old students with learning disorders gain a better understanding of their personal strengths and weaknesses. They see that learning styles vary greatly and find specific ways to approach work and manage the struggles that may beset them in school. Dr. Levine's helpful book is intended to convince students that the struggle is worth the effort and will ultimately be rewarding.

All Kinds of Minds
Mel Levine, M.D.

Young students with learning disorders--children in primary and elementary grades--can now gain insight into the difficulties they face in school. This book helps all children understand and respect all kinds of minds and can encourage children with learning disorders to maintain their motivation and keep from developing behavior problems stemming from their learning disorders. Ages 7-10.

My Brother's A World-Class Pain: A Sibling's Guide to ADHD
Michael Gordon, Ph.D.
This is the first book written for the oft-forgotten group of those affected by ADD: the brothers and sisters of ADD children. While they frequently bear the brunt of the ADD child's impulsiveness and distractibility, siblings usually are not afforded opportunities to understand the nature of the problem and to have their own feelings and thoughts addressed. This story about an older sister's efforts to deal with her active and impulsive brother sends the clear message to siblings of the ADD child that they can play an important role in a family's quest for change.

It's Just Attention Disorder: A Video Guide for Kids
Sam Goldstein, Ph.D. and Michael Goldstein, M.D.
Accurate diagnosis for ADD has become a reality and now the next step becomes treatment. To be helped, ADD children and adolescents must want help. *It's Just Attention Disorder* was created to help parents, teachers, and counselors assist the ADD child and adolescent to become an active participant in the treatment process. Filmed in an "MTV" format, this video will hold the attention of even the most inattentive. It has been designed to acquaint the ADD child and adolescent with basic information concerning the nature and treatment of ADD. Included with the video are a User's Manual and Study Guide.

I Would If I Could: A Teenager's Guide to ADHD/Hyperactivity
Michael Gordon, Ph.D.
Dr. Gordon has written a compelling book especially for the adolescent with ADHD. This book not only provides straightforward information about ADHD, but also explores its impact on family relationships, self-esteem, and friendships. The use of humor and candor help educate and encourage teenagers who too often, find themselves confused and frustrated.

To order any of the above or additional resources contact:
A.D.D. WareHouse
(800) 233-9273

Books and Videos for Parents and Teachers

Barkley, R. A. (1990). Attention Deficit Hyperactivity Disorder: A Handbook for Diagnosis and Treatment. New York: Guilford Press.

Barkley, R.A. (1992) ADHD: What Do We Know? New York: Guilford Press (Video).

Barkley, R.A. (1992) ADHD: What Can We Do? New York: Guilford Press (Video).

Brooks, R. (1991) The Self-Esteem Teacher. Minnesota: American Guidance Service.

Fowler, M. (1993). Maybe You Know My Kid. New York: Carol Publishing Group.

Fowler, M. (1992) CH.A.D.D. Educators Manual. Florida: CH.A.D.D..

Goldstein S., & Goldstein, M. (1989).Why Won't My Child Pay Attention? Utah: Neurology, Learning and Behavior Center (Video).

Goldstein, S., & Goldstein, M. (1990). Educating Inattentive Children. Utah: Neurology, Learning and Behavior Center (Video).

Goldstein S., & Goldstein, M. (1992). Hyperactivity: Why Won't My Child Pay Attention? New York: John Wiley & Sons.

Gordon, M. (1991). ADHD/Hyperactivity: A Consumer's Guide. New York: GSI Publications.

Greenberg, G. & Horn, W. (1991) ADHD: Questions and Answers. Illinois: Research Press.

Hallowell, E. & Ratey, J. (1994) Driven to Distraction. New York: Pantheon.

Ingersoll, B. (1988). Your Hyperactive Child: A Parent's Guide to Coping with Attention Deficit Disorder. New York: Doubleday.

Ingersoll, B. & Goldstein, S. (1993). Attention Deficit Disorder and Learning Disabilities: Realities, Myths and Controversial Treatments. New York: Bantam Doubleday Dell.

Latham, P. S. and Latham, P. H. (1993) Attention Deficit Disorder and the Law. Washington, D.C.: JKL Communications.

Parker, H. (1990). Listen, Look, and Think. Plantation, Florida: Specialty Press, Inc.

Parker, H. (1991) The Goal Card Program. Plantation, Florida: Specialty Press, Inc.

Parker, H. (1992). The ADD Hyperactivity Handbook for Schools. Plantation, Florida: Specialty Press, Inc.

Parker, H. (1992). The ADAPT Program. Plantation, Florida: Specialty Press, Inc.

Phelan, T. (1984). 1-2-3 Magic! Training Your Preschoolers and Preteens to Do What You Want. Illinois: Child Management.

Phelan, T. (1984). 1-2-3 Magic! Training Your Preschoolers and Preteens to Do What You Want. Illinois: Child Management (Video).

Phelan, T. (1984). All About Attention Deficit Disorder. Illinois: Child Management.

Phelan, T. (1993). All About Attention Deficit Disorder. Illinois: Child Management (Video).

Phelan, T. (1991). Surviving Your Adolescents. Illinois: Child Management.

Kelly, K. and Ramundo, P. (1992) You Mean I'm Not Lazy, Stupid or Crazy?! Tyrell & Jerem Press.

Rief, S. (1993). How to Reach and Teach ADD/ADHD Children. New York: Center for Applied Research in Education.

Silver, L. (1984). The Misunderstood Child: A Guide for Parents of LD Children. New York: McGraw Hill.

Silver, L (1993). Dr. Larry Silver's Advice to Parents on Attention-Deficit Hyperactivity Disorder. Washington, D.C.: American Psychiatric Press.

Weiss, L. (1992). Attention Deficit Disorder in Adults. Dallas, Texas: Taylor Publishing Company.

Wender, P. H. (1987). The Hyperactive Child, Adolescent, and Adult: Attention Deficit Disorder Through the Life Span. New York: Oxford University Press.

Resources for Families and Professionals

**Children and Adults with Attention Deficit Disorders
CH.A.D.D.**
Suite 109
499 Northwest 70th Avenue
Plantation, Florida 33317
(305) 587-3700

**Learning Disabilities Association of America
LDA**
4156 Library Road
Pittsburgh, Pennsylvania 15234
(412) 341-1515

**National Information Center for Handicapped Children and
Youth**
P.O. Box 1492
Washington, D.C. 20013

Orton Dyslexia Society
Chester Building
Suite 382
8600 LaSalle Road
Baltimore, Maryland 21204
(800) 222-3132

Tourette Syndrome Association
42-40 Bell Boulevard
Bayside, New York 11361
(800) 237-0717

Appendix A

Charts, Rating Scales and
Sticker Contracts for Parents and Kids

Page

Sticker Chart Contract

You will get a sticker every time you _____

_____

However, if you misbehave then _____

_____

When you get _____ stickers on your chart you can _____

good Bedtime Behavior

Sticker Chart Contract

You will get a sticker every time you _____
_____

However, if you misbehave then _____
_____

When you get _____ stickers on your chart you can _____

GOOD BEHAVIOR IN PUBLIC

RICE

SUGAR

CEREAL

SOAP

Peas

MEALTIME MANNERS

Sticker Chart Contract

You will get a sticker every time you _____

_____.

However, if you misbehave then _____

_____.

When you get _____ stickers on your chart you can _____

Sticker Chart Contract

You will get a sticker every time you _____

_____

However, if you misbehave then _____

_____

When you get _____ stickers on your chart you can _____

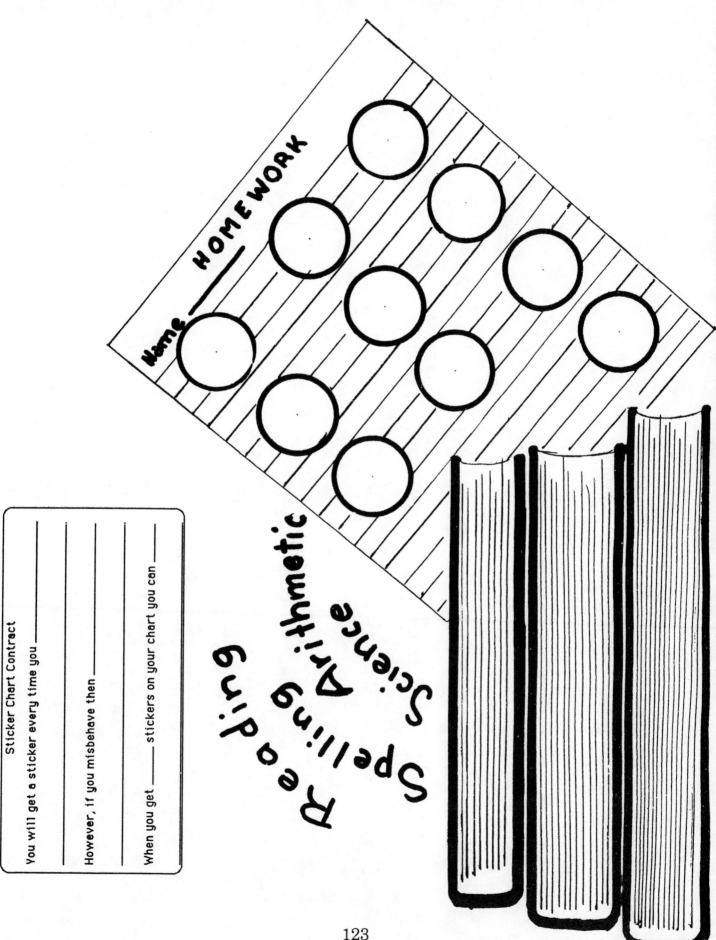

HOMEWORK

Name

Reading
Spelling
Arithmetic
Science

Sticker Chart Contract

You will get a sticker every time you _____

However, if you misbehave then _____

When you get _____ stickers on your chart you can _____

Sticker Chart Contract

You will get a sticker every time you _____

_____

However, if you misbehave then _____

_____

When you get _____ stickers on your chart you can _____

Let's Get Ready

Let's Get Ready to Read!

Sticker Chart Contract

You will get a sticker every time you _____

However, if you misbehave then _____

When you get _____ stickers on your chart you can _____

Be a Safe Car Rider

TREATMENT EVALUATION RECORD

Child:		Age:	Teacher:	

AGE IN YEARS	ATRS CUT-OFF SCORES BOYS GIRLS	MEDICATION DOSAGE & ATRS SCORES		
		DATE _____ DOSE _____	DATE _____ DOSE _____	DATE _____ DOSE _____
6-8	18 13			
9-11	20 14			
12-14	13 7			
15-17	13 16			

Note: Please note medication name and dosage in mg.. Note if medication is taken more than once per day. Note any observable side effects here:

- -

TREATMENT EVALUATION RECORD

Child:		Age:	Teacher:	

AGE IN YEARS	ATRS CUT-OFF SCORES BOYS GIRLS	MEDICATION DOSAGE & ATRS SCORES		
		DATE _____ DOSE _____	DATE _____ DOSE _____	DATE _____ DOSE _____
6-8	18 13			
9-11	20 14			
12-14	13 7			
15-17	13 16			

Note: Please note medication name and dosage in mg.. Note if medication is taken more than once per day. Note any observable side effects here:

PRESCHOOL & KINDERGARTEN
GOAL CARD PROGRAM (P)rimary

CHILD'S NAME _____ TEACHER_____

WEEK OF _____

GOAL CARD

	MON	TUE	WED	THU	FRI
PAID ATTENTION					
PLAYED NICELY					
FOLLOWED RULES					
TOTAL					

1 = TRY HARDER

2 = BETTER

3 = GREAT JOB

MY GOAL IS TO
GET ____ POINTS

- -

CHILD'S NAME _____ TEACHER_____

WEEK OF _____

GOAL CARD

	MON	TUE	WED	THU	FRI
PAID ATTENTION					
PLAYED NICELY					
FOLLOWED RULES					
TOTAL					

1 = TRY HARDER

2 = BETTER

3 = GREAT JOB

MY GOAL IS TO
GET ____ POINTS

PRESCHOOL & KINDERGARTEN
GOAL CARD PROGRAM (P)rimary

CHILD'S NAME _____ TEACHER_____

WEEK OF _____

GOAL CARD

	MON	TUE	WED	THU	FRI
PAID ATTENTION					
PLAYED NICELY					
FOLLOWED RULES					
TOTAL					

1 = TRY HARDER

2 = BETTER

3 = GREAT JOB

MY GOAL IS TO
GET ____ POINTS

- -

CHILD'S NAME _____ TEACHER_____

WEEK OF _____

GOAL CARD

	MON	TUE	WED	THU	FRI
PAID ATTENTION					
PLAYED NICELY					
FOLLOWED RULES					
TOTAL					

1 = TRY HARDER

2 = BETTER

3 = GREAT JOB

MY GOAL IS TO
GET ____ POINTS